A Hospital Chaplain at the Crossroads of Humanity

Rev. Bill Alberts

Rev. William E. Alberts, Ph.D.

March 2012

All names have been changed to protect the identity of patients and their families.

Dedication

This book is dedicated to my wife, Eva, whose own experience at the crossroads of life, perceptive editorial touch, and empowering encouragement have helped to illuminate the crossroads of patients and their families herein.

Table of Contents

Foreword 8

Comments From A Medical Doctor 11

Comments From A Professor Of Urban And Environmental Policy & Planning 13

Acknowledgements 14

Introduction 16

1. "Hug her" 18

2. The Humanness In Front Of Us 21

3. Sweatshirt 'Jesus' 24

4. "Thank you for staying with us." 26

5. "And say my name, too" 29

6. "I want to get tight with him" 32

7. "Little Things Mean A Lot" 34

8. "You could have written my name on a blackboard, and I wouldn't have known it" 37

9. "You gave me my humanity" 38

10. A Prayer And A Paper 40

11. "I should have done more for him" 42

12. The Rainbow Itself Is The Pot Of Gold 44

13. "Jesus and I travel light" 46

14. "In the zone" 48

15. "What do you tell someone who is going to die?" 50

16. When You Start Off On The Wrong Foot 52

17. "Pray that I win the lottery" 55

18. The Various Ways In Which The Human Spirit Moves Its Wonders To Perform 57

19. Out Of The Mouth Of Babes... And Older People 59

20. Caring Is About Timing—And Embracing The Unexpected 61

21. "I know who I am" 63

22. "Could you say a prayer for me?" 66

23. 24/7 68

24. Honoring Diversity In Patient Care 69

25. "What does she want on it?" 72

26. "You're scaring me" 74

27. Chaplaincy Is About Helping Patients *Get* Better, Not *Be* Better 76

28. The Empowerment Of Being Understood 79

29. "Exceptional Care" In The Cafeteria And The Chapel 81

30. "I'm sorry to go on like this, chaplain. You probably came to talk about the church." 83

31. "I was a hopeless drug addict. Now I'm a dopeless hope addict." 85

32. "Will it cost us more to have you come back a second time?" 88

33. "I'm so thankful you are here" 90

34. On Being Imperfect 92

35. Of Tattoos And Love 94

36. On Getting Close To People 96

37. The "Snot-Nosed Kid" Who Was Loved 98

38. "This has been a pleasant surprise... Your Excellency" 100

39. "Take off your hats" 102

40. "I miss her so bad." 105

41. "Are you affiliated with a religion?" "No, I'm free." 108

42. Pastoral Care By Ear And Sight 111

43. "I told God I needed a real flesh and blood angel" 114

44. "For the longest time" 117

45. "No preference" 120

46. "Here comes the bill collector" 122

47. "Would you bless this crucifix for me?" 124

48. Go Down Kicking 126

49. It Is About Kindness 129

50. "I'll take what you've got" 132

51. Homeless But Not Loveless 134

52. She Made Something Out Of Nothing 136

53. A Christmas Story: "Ah, I can see a little sparkle now" 138

54. An Invocation For The Holidays 140

Foreword

It has been over half a century since I served as a hospital chaplain and even then it was sort of incognito. As a doctoral student at Boston University, I had landed a part-time job as the Executive Secretary of the Institute of Pastoral Care, at the time one of the two major organizations providing Clinical Pastoral Education to seminarians. For a variety of reasons—mostly financial—the Institute had me share an office with the hospital chaplain of the Massachusetts General Hospital—rent free. Jim Burns was the chaplain and to say that he was overworked would be putting it mildly. Partly because of his work load, and noting that some days my administrative work for the Institute was light, he recruited me to call on patients "if I wanted to."

At the time I had had but one summer unit of Clinical Pastoral Education and from that experience decided that I wasn't about to switch from preparing for a teaching ministry in one of my denomination's colleges to that of a health care ministry in a general or mental hospital. That decision was enforced when one of the first patients Jim asked me to visit was a truck driver from Tennessee who, while driving through the city of Boston, developed severe back pains, serious enough to lead to his being hospitalized.

In those days a hospital chaplain wore a grey jacket quite similar to what physicians and orderlies wore except that on the chaplain's lapels were two silver crosses. So as I entered the truck driver's room, he stared at me—probably hoping I was a doctor—then quickly shifted his gaze to the silver crosses, and barked, "Now what the hell do you want?"

I was reminded of that ancient memory when William E. Alberts invited me to read *A Hospital Chaplain at the Crossroads of Humanity*, and as I read Bill's extraordinary accounts of some of his interactions with the thousands of patients he has served in his health care ministry, I could not help but wonder what my career decision might have been had I known, and truly internalized, Chaplain Alberts' rich notions of what hospital chaplaincy is all about.

Here is a sample of the "one-liners" that frequently summarize the specific events he has experienced and records with particular patients or their families:

"Chaplaincy is enabling patients and their loved ones to tell their stories, the telling of which is good for the soul—and the mind and body."

"Chaplaincy is about discovering the little things that mean a lot to patients and their loved ones."

"Chaplaincy is about both feet planted responsively amidst the realities and strengths and needs of patients and their loved ones."

"Chaplaincy, like any meaningful relationship, is about taking the time to respond to human need."

"Chaplaincy is about helping patients *get* better not *be* better."

"The bottom line of chaplaincy is not about belief but about caring for patients and their loved ones."

Each of these challenging snips is a generalization of a particular encounter Chaplain Alberts has had with a patient or with his or her family. And each one—it seems to me—could serve as a topic for theological, religious, and spiritual discussion, as well as a portrait of a contemporary hospital chaplain's work.

But even if one were not a chaplain or considering hospital chaplaincy as an expression of ministry, how the author visualizes pastoral care would be applicable to any priest, minister, rabbi, imam, or religious layperson desiring to authentically offer care to those in need.

Examples:

"Pastoral care is about being a witness to the pain and courage of human love."

"Pastoral care is about being fully present and staying with grieving loved ones—however long their need."

"Pastoral care is about remembering and saying people's names—not just about praying for them in another's name."

"Pastoral care is about enabling patients to tell their stories, the sharing of which affirms and empowers the teller and often provides wisdom for the listener."

"Pastoral care involves getting close to people. And getting close to people involves getting close to people."

"Pastoral care is about giving grief the hearing it needs rather than remaining bottled up and beside itself."

"Pastoral care is about embodying and facilitating and revering kindness."

9

In these times of technological innovations and electronic communications, human touch frequently takes a thorough thrashing. It may be that an authentic spiritual ministry—whether from a hospital chaplain or a parish pastor—is becoming one of a very few last opportunities to salvage and embrace a particular human encounter where empowerment, not the promotion of a particular world view or a narrow set of religious or political beliefs, permeates the human relationship. If that be so, then Chaplain Alberts' willingness to share his myriad patient encounters with those in pain, turmoil, and crisis can serve well as a guide for all of us who truly want to explore better ways to care.

> Orlo C. Strunk, Jr., Ph.D., D.D.
> Managing Editor Emeritus
> *The Journal of Pastoral Care & Counseling*

Comments from a Medical Doctor

As an internist at Doctor Alberts' home institution of Boston Medical Center, I read *A Hospital Chaplain at the Crossroads of Humanity* with great professional and personal interest. Doctor Alberts was a force for humanity at our inner-city hospital for over 18 years. Until his retirement in 2011, he was a friend and confidant to many of the staff, and a source of great comfort and support to innumerable patients and their families. Yet very few of us had insight into his work with our patients—what was said behind closed doors—and this reflection on a career in hospital chaplaincy provides just that.

Doctor Alberts' book is fundamentally about his approach to hospital chaplaincy, which is profoundly person-centered. He asserts in his introduction that chaplaincy is about "empowering patients . . . not imposing any belief or value system on them," and his book is a recollection of transformative moments during which quiet explorations of patients' values and concerns wound up being a powerful tonic.

In one such story, an elderly man told his palliative care nurse he'd soon be "shoveling coal." When Doctor Alberts visited him, he found the gentleman was convinced he'd soon be in hell. Doctor Alberts found he was able to bolster this man's sense of his own humanness and worth by assuring him that wherever he wound up after death, he'd be joining him. And that neither of them would be "shoveling coal." What reassured this patient was not prayer, Doctor Alberts writes, but someone who "not only voiced caring about whether he lived or died but caring for him even after he died. Doctor Alberts adds, "Though prayer to a loving god is often a powerful way to affirm and reassure a patients."

Perhaps the most poignant moments in this book are those in which Doctor Alberts writes of the wisdom gleaned from patients he has met. In one vignette, a Hindu gentleman with an inclusive world view comments that his own religious views defy definition, as "the eagle soars throughout the heavens—not just in one direction or another." In another story, a patient with a life-threatening illness reflects that a prolonged hospital stay doesn't clarify what is most important. Rather it leads one to believe that nothing in life isn't important. *A Hospital Chaplain at the Crossroads of Humanity* is a work brimming with humility and humanity. It is a beautiful, thoughtful and thought-provoking piece of writing. For those working in or considering a career in chaplaincy, it is a primer in how to stand with "both feet planted . . . amidst the realities and strengths and needs of patients and their loved ones." A starting point for those seeking to be more responsive to people seeking solace.

For medical professionals, reading this work provides an opportunity to reflect on and improve our interactions with patients. Doctor Alberts believes that religion should "help people perceive and deal with reality," while much of our struggle is to modify, if not cure, disease. There is, then, a fundamental difference in the work of the chaplain and the physician. Yet the challenging work we share is to "listen and respond to what patients are saying and not saying," and to find what "engages them and lifts their spirits." Doctor Alberts' beautiful book helps re-direct our interests and our efforts toward this crucial element in medical care. It is a "must read."

Michael D. Stillman, MD
Boston University Affiliated Physicians, Inc.

Comments from a Professor of Urban and Environmental Policy & Planning

US society continues to be engulfed in a national and momentous debate about the quality and access of health services for everyone. The debate is intense and will only become more so as recent enactments of universal health insurance are challenged by a range of interests. Rev. Alberts' collection of essays describing some of his personal experiences as a hospital chaplain at a major urban university medical center help to remind us that there are human faces to our debates about health. His essays reflect two important realities which should be integral to our national discourse about health. One reality is that health has a human face that should not be forgotten or ignored even in the face of onslaughts by technocrats and their hard numbers about profit bottom-lines in the health industries. A second reality is that health is a universal connector for all human beings. Regardless of one's racial or ethnic background, or one's creed, or gender, or sexual orientation, or age, when faced with health crisis there is a realization that none of these temporary divisions really matter. Thoughtfully, and eloquently, Rev. Alberts' essays about real people and the health situations and crises they faced illustrate these two realities. This short and powerful book should be widely read by everyone, including those charged with delivering health to all of us, but especially by those persons in leadership positions who can help determine the direction and scope, *and decency*, of our nation's health system.

James Jennings, Ph.D
Tufts University

Acknowledgements

I am most fortunate and deeply grateful to have been a hospital chaplain at Boston Medical Center for eighteen-and-a-half years—a hospital whose inclusiveness is celebrated in its mission to provide "Exceptional Care. Without Exception." A hospital whose honoring of diversity in patient care is reflected in the pride it takes in the diversity of its staff of caregivers.

I have been privileged to know and interact with so many nurses, doctors, social workers and various other multidisciplinary staff and support persons, whose assistance and expertise have contributed immeasurably to my pastoral care of patients and their loved ones.

Special tribute is made here to my colleagues in Boston Medical Center's Pastoral Care Department: staff chaplain Rev. Dr. Jennie Gould; Catholic Chaplains Sr. Maryanne Ruzzo, Fr. Roger Bourgea and Fr. John Murphy; Jewish Chaplain Rabbi Paul Levenson; former Muslim Chaplain Salih Yucel; former longtime Director of Pastoral Care Mary Chin, MSW; current Director and Vice Chair of Clinical Psychiatry Peggy Johnson, M.D.; and Pastoral Care and Social Work Departments' Administrative Manager Susan Tofuri. Their collegiality, competence and caring of patients have greatly enriched my chaplaincy over all these years.

Deep appreciation is also extended to the College of Pastoral Supervision and Psychotherapy (CPSP), a chaplaincy-certifying clinical pastoral education (CPE) training body of which I have been a Diplomate in Pastoral Psychotherapy since 1997. The value CPSP places on the relationships between us chaplains ourselves, and on our personal authority, creativity and accountability have added much affirmation, insight, grace and empowerment to my chaplaincy and related writings.

I am deeply thankful for the collegiality of Rev. Dr. Perry Miller, Editor of *Pastoral Report*, The Newsletter of CPSP. He is Director of the Pastoral Care and Counseling Institute in Durham, NC, a North Carolina Board Certified Psychotherapist and Clinical Supervisor, as well as a Diplomate in Clinical Pastoral Supervision and Psychotherapy in the College of Pastoral Supervision and Psychotherapy. The book has come into being primarily because Perry has published a number of the stories herein in *Pastoral Report*, believes the stories would offer a valuable resource in the clinical pastoral training of theological students and active clergy, and thus encouraged me to write the book.

Thanks also to Maria Pantages Ober, Interim Director of Corporate Communications at Boston Medical Center and Boston University Medical Campus. Maria read and cleared the stories herein to protect the right of privacy of patients and their families—and on occasion provided refinement with her strong editorial skills.

I am very grateful to Boston Medical Center hospital staff chaplain Dr. Samuel Lowe for his careful proofing of the manuscript.

Much appreciation is extended to Krista Argiropolis, director of Oak Hill Office Solutions, for her expert compilation and creative formatting of the manuscript for publication.

Special appreciation is extended to Boston Medical Center's patients and their loved ones. They welcomed me into their lives with trust, and shared their stories. Stories filled with tears and laughter, wisdom and faith. Stories echoing a common humanity across diverse belief, culture, ideology, and nationality. The patients and their families have greatly enriched my life, and deepened my appreciation of the diversity and commonality of the human community. This book is dedicated to them—and to all the staff who care for them at Boston Medical Center's crossroads of humanity.

What, for me, began as an outward calling to the ministry sixty-two years ago became an inward journey into self. My deep thanks to so many persons who contributed to that journey—and thus to the patients' stories that follow.

Introduction

A hospital is a unique crossroads of humanity, and therefore calls for pastoral care that is comfortable with and accepting of diversity of belief and non-belief. I see patients as representing the diversity of divinity and the divinity of diversity—and the commonality of humanity.

For me, the pastoral care of hospital patients begins with the humanness of the chaplain. The inward journey where one becomes self-aware, and is in touch with and accepting of oneself. The more such self-awareness the better prepared one is to understand and accept patients and their loved ones as themselves, and to experience their reality not interpret it. We chaplains have to know where we—and our god—are coming from in order to know where patients and their families—and their god—are at. Self-knowledge helps one avoid the counter-transference of getting in one's own way in living and working with and providing care for people.

Pastoral/spiritual care, therefore, is not about the chaplain but about the patient. It is about the chaplain in terms of his or her awareness that it is about the patient. Thus pastoral/spiritual care is not about what the chaplain has to bestow on the patient, but about what the patient has to share regarding his or her reality. Chaplaincy is about empowering patients and their families, not imposing any belief or value system on them. It is about empathy, not evangelism. About connecting with, not converting. Empowering, not gaining power over. Respect for the patient's beliefs and rights is fundamental. This emphasis is not to minimize the identity and faith of the chaplain. Rather, it is to stress the pastoral/spiritual care qualities of self-awareness and inner emotional security that enable the chaplain to allow patients and their families, to be who they are.

Self-awareness and emotional security free a chaplain to join in an interdisciplinary commitment to fulfill any hospital's mission of providing "Exceptional Care. Without Exception" (Boston Medical Center's stated mission). Every hospital individualizes the patients and puts the well-being and rights of each at the center of health care. Thus a chaplain's work is determined by the expressed beliefs, wishes and spiritual and human needs of patients and their loved ones. It is about utilizing and reinforcing patients' and families' beliefs in their efforts and struggles to recover or to cope with dying and loss and grief.

A hospital especially reveals humanity's commonality as well as it's diversity. Illness confronts all people with their mortality and hence their vulnerability, their humanness—their oneness and connectedness with each other. In a hospital, the common humanity people share comes to the fore and tends to transcend their differences. Here there is the pronounced mutual sharing of struggles with life and death, hope and fear, pain and anguish, love and anger, joy and sadness. And it is these very struggles that bring out the tremendous wisdom patients and their families possess. The role of pastoral care is to affirm these common human struggles -- and the wisdom they elicit -- by giving them air and reverence.

The hospital is an exceptional crossroads of humanity. It is actually a global neighborhood, and therefore calls for a chaplain who embraces diversity of belief-- "without exception." *Chaplains without theological blinders.* The stories herein are about the struggles and wisdom and faith of people who enter the especially humanizing crossroads of this global neighborhood.

1. "Hug her"

"Lift her up, Lord! Take that fluid from her body. I'm going to keep on praying to you day and night . . . Almighty God, make her well. Which will be a great testimony to you for all patients and doctors and nurses to see." These were prayers of the sister of a 47-year-old black Baptist woman who was critically ill with cancer.

This loving sister and family saw me, as hospital chaplain, being sent by their god to help "raise up" their loved one to renewed health. "Every time she has to go for a test, you come through the door," the sister said, "and you say a prayer, and she gets a little better." Again, "You always come at the right time. Pray that her oxygen level goes up." Later, even the patient's uncle greeted me with, "The last time you prayed her kidneys opened up."

On another occasion, the intubated and medicated patient's sister and a female friend were clapping their hands and singing to her: "What a mighty God! He will raise you up!" And when the patient slowly opened her eyes in response, the sister excitedly pointed to her face, and they clapped and sang all the louder: "What a mighty god! He will raise you up!" Then they yelled to her, "Fight it, Martha! Fight it, Martha!" Afterwards, I asked the patient's nurse whether such loud singing and clapping might not be helpful to the patient. The nurse took care of my concern with, "They need to be in the room with her."

During another visit, the patient's sister said to me, "She's going to make it. She's a tough cookie." I responded, "You are always here for her." The sister replied, "She's always been there for us."

The patient's partner of many years was like-minded in his religious belief. He was at the patient's bedside daily, and often stayed through the night. He believed "God is going to help her get out of here the way she came in." I looked at the weakened, intubated, apparently dying patient, and wondered if my presence and prayers might be reinforcing this loving family's need to deny the pain of reality. Still, I was not about to pull the rug of denial out from under

18

their faith. I wanted to continue being there to support them when reality might hit.

Aware of the patient's medically diagnosed critical condition, my requested prayers focused on the abiding shepherd-like care of the family's god for their loved one, the strength she found in her faith, the deep love she and her family shared, and thankfulness for her good work in training public school teachers in their work with children and parents. I also repeated words from her sister's spoken prayers, offered before mine-- a sibling's prayers that contained very human, insightful, and loving references.

The family's faith in their god's healing power came through very clearly at a family meeting. The medical team told the patient's family that they had done all they could for the patient. The response of the patient's twenty-some-years-old son and spokesperson was, "My mother told me not to give up on her. 'Don't let them pull the plug on me,' she said to me." He continued, "She's a fighter, and she wants a fighting chance. And that's the kind of belief we have in God. She taught me that." There was this mutual understanding: the medical team had done all it could; now the family members turned completely to their god. Two weeks later the patient died.

An early morning page informed me of the patient's death, and when I arrived at the hospital, her mother and sister were in her room. When I expressed sorrow, her mother said that her daughter was not dead. I went to the patient's bedside, and stood across from her sister, who tearfully asked me to offer a prayer. "Don't you say no prayer for the dead," her mother declared. "She's not dead. She is living." The sister asked me to "say a live prayer," which I did.

The mother was in denial. She came over to her dead daughter's beside, pulled up the cover, felt her foot and said, "She's not dead." The mother then put her hand on her dead daughter's forehead and prayed loudly, "In the name of Jesus! In the name of Jesus! Raise her up, Lord! In the name of Jesus!" A few minutes later the sister read aloud the 23rd Psalm over her dead sister.

Later, more family members arrived, and they began to make plans for the removal of the patient's body to a funeral home. At one point, the mother's brother said to the patient's sister (his niece), "What do you want me to do with your mother?" His niece replied, "Hug her." He shrugged, and said, "Oh, come on. Shouldn't we involve her in the planning?" She replied, "Yes. And then hug her."

The patient's son was the last to arrive. He went to her bedside, with tears in his eyes, and stood silently looking at her. A moment later, as the patient's sister was about to speak to him, she stopped herself, seeing that his eyes were closed and that he was possibly saying a prayer. She waited until he opened his eyes to speak to him. As the son continued to stand by his mother's body, his grandmother came over to him and evidently repeated to him that his mother was not dead. He reacted, "Grandma, please! She's dead!" Tears then streamed down his face. And his grandmother walked away.

Later I followed the son out of his mother's room—remembering him saying that his mother told him not to give up on or let the plug be pulled on her, that she was a fighter, and that such determination is part of their religious faith, which she taught him. I went up to him, and hugged him and expressed sympathy and said, "You are a very loving son." I continued, "As you said, your mother is a fighter; and she fought very hard; and you gave her every chance." "Thank you," he replied, and returned my hug.

The son had assumed a heavy burden of responsibility for his mother's care. My aim was to affirm his steadfast devotion to her, and help to relieve any possible guilt he may have felt.

Pastoral care is about being a witness to the pain and courage of human love: "Grandma, please! She's dead!" It is also about being present to family love that says about the one who needs it most, "Hug her."

2. The Humanness In Front Of Us

My daily work begins with visiting patients, whose religion is unknown, obtaining their affiliation, and, if affiliated, making that information known to the appropriate chaplains. These patients especially provide examples of the spontaneous humanness one encounters as a hospital chaplain.

Like the 78-year old white male patient in an intensive care unit, whose religion was listed as "unknown" I entered his room and introduced myself as the hospital chaplain making my rounds on the floor. He interrupted, "I can't hear, and I had cataracts and can't see." I crossed the room, walked around to the upper side of his bed and said, more loudly, "I'm Rev. Alberts, hospital chaplain, making my rounds." Before I could state the purpose of my routine visit, he shouted, "*I don't want any religious person in my room!*"

The patient's outburst surprised me. But my surprise was tempered by my belief that patients may have a good reason for reacting negatively to a "religious person." Moving away from his bedside, I replied, "You answered my question" [about whether he had a religious affiliation]. Then, reaching for something in common with him, I said, "I recently had cataracts removed from my eyes." He replied, "I had one removed, and that is why I'm blind." "I'm sorry," I said, heading toward the door, and adding, "I respect your wishes very much." "That's okay," he replied, his tone positive. Then he asked, "Could you do something for me?" "Sure," I answered, surprised again. "Push that table [his over-bed mobile table] closer so I can reach that ginger ale and cup," he directed. He then commented, "These freakin' people don't know what they're doing. I have a bum right shoulder and can't reach it, and the table is too far away from my other hand."

The patient's predicament was obvious, and his frustration understandable. I pushed the table closer to him, and handed him the cup. He drank what was left in it, pulled the straw from the can of ginger ale and said, "That straw doesn't work either." He proceeded to pour ginger ale into the cup and drink it. Then, after a pause, he said, "Thank you. You've been a big help to me." "You're welcome," I replied. It was about him having access to ginger ale and not to a god. The humanness in front of us.

For another patient, it was about his needing access to a loving god. An older, terminally ill black man, the patient told a palliative care nurse that soon he would be "shoveling coal." The concerned nurse shared his troubling words of self-condemnation with me, said he was dying of cancer, had difficulty speaking because of his weakened condition, and asked that I visit him. His doctor also told me "We're in a muddle about his saying he's going to shovel coal in the next life, not knowing how to handle it."

The patient confirmed that he was "going to be shoveling a lot of coal" when he died. Why? "Because of the number of bad things I have done in my life," he said in a weakened tone. I did not pursue the "bad things" he said he did because of his difficulty speaking. Instead, I asked him if anyone had ever done "bad things" to him "growing up and in your life?" "Yes, a lot."

Having researched and written about America's white-controlled hierarchy of access to economic and political power, I assumed he probably had at least two racial strikes waiting for him when he was born. One invisible strike could be seen in a study that found, "Blacks Suffer Heart Failure More Than Whites . . . at a rate 20 times higher than did whites, even dying of it decades before the condition typically strikes whites . . . researchers reported." (*The New York Times*, Mar. 19, 2009)

The second unseen strike against this patient may be found in another recent study that showed, "Chronic stress from growing up poor appears to have a direct impact on the brain, leaving children with impairment in at least one key area—working memory." The "bad things" here: "Children raised in poverty suffer many ill effects: They often have health problems and tend to struggle in school, which can create a cycle of poverty across generations." (*The Boston Globe*, Apr. 7, 2009).

Sadly the patient had a self-loathing heart. A white-dominated hierarchy, with him at the bottom where "bad" economic and social and political and legal "things" happen to poor people of color especially—and also to economically strapped white persons. "Bad things" *legitimized* by a theology of self-hatred, which was *the third strike* that apparently led this patient to believe he would be "shoveling coal" in hell when he died. An apparently fundamentalist Christian theology of self-hatred, internalized through identification with parental and other religious authorities, many of whom are themselves possibly struggling with their own marginalization at the bottom of society. A theology of self-hatred born of oppressed and oppressive human relationships. A fundamentalist theology in which all persons, black and white alike, are born in sin, and will be "shoveling coal" unless they renounce their sinful nature and accept "Jesus Christ as the only Son of God and their Lord and Savior," who is portrayed as having died on the cross for their sins.

The citing of this substitutionary theology of atonement is not meant to disregard the model of Jesus as liberator, whom others believe was crucified on a Roman cross for seeking to set his Jewish people free from Roman occupation and oppression. The civil rights movement in America in black churches has found empowerment in Jesus' words, "The spirit of the Lord is upon me, because he has anointed me to preach good news to the poor . . . and to set at liberty those who are oppressed." (Luke 4: 18)

What may have reassured this patient was not so much my saying that Jesus revealed a "god of love who especially loves you." Nor my statement that all of us are human and in need of grace. Nor the fact that a lot of "bad things" had happened to him already. Nor even the prayer that I offered, though prayer to a loving god is often a powerful way to affirm and reassure a patient.

What seemed to especially connect with this patient was my telling him, "Wherever you are I will see you there." "You will?," he asked. "Yes, I'll be there. And neither of us will be shoveling coal." "I hope you're right," he said. Before his discharge to a hospice I saw him again and repeated: "Wherever you go, I'll be there. I'll look for you until I find you." "Okay," he replied. "That's a promise." "That's a promise," I said. The patient seemed to find reassurance in hearing someone not only voice caring about whether he lived or died but caring about him *even after he died.* The bottom line of pastoral care is *caring.*

The humanness in front of us. The humanness inside of us.

3. Sweatshirt 'JESUS'

His sweatshirt was to tell me a lot. Written across the front of it, in bold letters, was the word 'JESUS.' He is the husband of a 72-year-old white, evangelical Christian, intensive care unit patient. Upon entering her room and introducing myself, I turned to him and said, "I see you and Jesus are close." Both he and his wife were about to tell me how to grow human beings, whether it be a congregation, or a family, or even a community.

"Oh, yes, Jesus and I do have a lot in common," he replied. He then referred to his "non-denominational" and "Bible-based" church that started with 24 people less than ten years ago, and now has 800 members. The church began in rented space in a school, and, as the congregation grew by leaps and bounds, they bought a warehouse, and turned it into an 800-seat sanctuary, and a cafeteria, and rooms for meetings.

"A cafeteria?" I responded, surprised. "Yes," he said. "People can come on a Sunday morning and share an inexpensive breakfast, and then stay for the services. It's a lot more convenient than preparing a meal at home or eating out." His wife followed up by saying that he himself is a cook, and often helps prepare the breakfasts.

Fascinated by a church that could grow from 24 to 800 members within ten years, I asked them what led to such amazing growth. The patient herself responded, "It's because people in the church say to visitors, 'How can we help you?' It is about being a family," she continued. "Making people feel at home, and caring for one another."

I asked what kind of programs the church has that offer such caring. It was the husband's turn to respond: "We have a money management team that helps people who need advice about budgets and other financial matters. We also help people find jobs," he went on. "We have a marital counseling program, and a program for teens. We have outreach programs that include visiting nursing homes and providing music and prayers. And," he added, "we even provide breakfast on occasion for nursing home staff, so that they can take a break," explaining that some of the staff are church members.

The patient herself summed it up: "It is about looking after one another. You're not alone." She concluded, "It's different than just attending a Sunday service, and then getting up from the pew and going home, which is what we used to do." The fact that their church provides programs that seek to address people's economic needs during the current financial crisis says much about their 'JESUS' being down to earth.

It is about chaplaincy enabling patients and their loved ones to tell their stories, the telling of which is good for the soul—and the mind and body.

4. "Thank you for staying with us."

In answering a page, a chaplain never knows when he or she is going to be thrust into the middle of unexpected death and overwhelming grief. A 62-year-old Latino patient died suddenly following surgery, and her son and his wife and the patient's sister were devastated. When I arrived in the intensive care unit's small conference room, the patient's son and her sister were present and being comforted by staff—with the aide of an interpreter, as the sister spoke only Spanish, thus the conversation between her and the son was in Spanish.

Where does one begin? I don't speak Spanish. A staff member helped, by introducing me to them and telling me the son's name, and that he is a pastor. I then began with the son and his aunt, who were sitting next to each other. Standing behind them at that moment, I put my hands on their shoulders and listened as they spoke to each other and to staff and cried. The son, who, along with his wife, speaks English, stopped crying, looked at me and said about his mother, "She is in a better place now." He repeated this statement, naturally wanting to reassure himself, and resumed crying. He then stopped, looked at me again, and said, "She is at peace. She is with God." He then bowed his head over the conference room table, and began crying again. Staff members reassured him and his aunt that his mother did not suffer before she died.

The son's religious-oriented words led me to ask if he would like me to offer a prayer, which he did. My prayer began with his and his aunt's tears, which were the outpouring of their pain born of their love for mother and sister. Tears which their god sees and understands. The prayer also expressed the son's belief in a god of love who provides "a better place" for his mother to rest in peace. The prayer also initially provided me with a concrete vehicle on which to begin hanging my pastoral care, a vehicle also for communicating an understanding of their deep feelings of loss.

I felt comfortable with this family, staying with them for three-

26

and-a-half hours, during which they spoke mostly Spanish to each other. I listened and observed intently and responded to their universal language of love and grief.

First the aunt. When a nurse asked if the family members would like to see the patient, the aunt was the only one who did. And when I offered, she wanted me to go with her. I put my arm around her and escorted her to her sister's room, with the interpreter accompanying us. When she entered the room and saw her sister, she broke down and wept over her sister's body, stroking and kissing her face and expressing her love and sadness. Earlier a staff person recalled that the sister stayed with the patient all last evening, and helped her to bathe in preparation for her surgery. Through the interpreter, I verbalized the preciousness of the sisters' love for each other.

Shortly after we returned to the small conference room, the sister took two or three pills from a little container, looking at me as I watched, and swallowed them. She then continued looking at me, with a knowing raising of her eyebrows and a fleeting smile. I did not speak Spanish, nor she English, but our non-verbal language was on the same human wave length.

Later, when the son and I were alone in the conference room, he unburdened himself. "I have never lost anyone close to me," he said. "How will I feel tomorrow? Can you tell me?" "You will still love your mother tomorrow," I said. "Yes," he replied. "And tomorrow you will still feel the pain of your grief," I continued. "In time, the grief will still be there, but the ache will lessen." "Have you ever lost a loved one?" he asked. "Yes," I replied. "My father and mother, and four brothers, and a sister."

"Will I be able to continue my ministry?" he asked. "Yes. And your grief will help you understand others even more. And you will have an even deeper love, and for more people. For all people lose loved ones and grieve," I continued. "It is part of who all of us are as human beings." He nodded with an understanding smile.

The son is the minister of music of his church, a newly formed, small, evangelical congregation of a year—he had previously served 14 years as minister of music of a larger church in another state. Along with directing the choir, he plays the piano, trumpet and guitar. His enjoyment in talking about his specialized ministry was seen in him repeating to me with a smile, "God loves music." I enthusiastically agreed.

Along with our extended conversation, I continued sitting beside the son when he called and talked with his grandfather, and then his father—both in their native country in South America. "Yes, papi." "Yes, papi," the son repeatedly said to his father, with telephone in one hand and his head resting in the other hand, and wiping away tears from his eyes. Love of a father and son that affirms and remembers and comforts and strengthens. In between calls, the son looked at me and said, "Thank you for staying with us." "You're most welcome," I replied.

When present, the son's wife constantly comforted him, hugging and kissing and reassuring him. And his aunt also hugged and kissed him, and spoke words of comfort to him.

A major concern of all three was the son's older brother, whom they described as being very emotional, and who would be arriving at the hospital soon with his wife. As we waited for their arrival, the son's wife said words similar to her husband's: "Thank you for staying with us all this time."

As soon as the older brother and his wife arrived, he looked into his younger brother's eyes, and knew that their mother had died. They moved quickly to each other, and hugged each other tightly, at length, and cried. Then the brothers' wives and their aunt encircled and hugged them—with us hospital staff persons reaching out and joining their circle of grief and love.

Pastoral care is about listening and feeling, as well as talking. It has a universal human language: it is about being fully present and staying with grieving loved ones-- however long their need.

5. "And say my name, too"

She was a black patient in her forties whose religion was listed "No Affiliation." I introduced myself as hospital chaplain making my rounds, and asked if she were affiliated with a religion. She said that her mother was a Jehovah's Witness and that she wanted the hospital to also list her that way. When I said, "May the blessings of Jehovah be yours," she thanked me, and held out her hand to shake mine. She then asked, "What's your name?" I repeated, "Bill Alberts, hospital chaplain." She then said, "Will you keep me in your prayers?" "Yes," I replied, and then asked, "Would you like me to offer a prayer now?" "No," she said. "Just keep me in your prayers. *And say my name, too.* My mother said it's all right to say my name." "I sure will," I replied. "Your name is precious to Jehovah." "I'll keep you in my prayers, too," she responded. "Thank you," I said. "I appreciate that."

It was not just about prayer. Nor about spirituality. Nor even about Jehovah. It was even more about saying her *name.* It was about *her.* And about my *name.* About *me.* Pastoral care is about *remembering* and *saying* people's names. Far more than praying to or in the name of . . . It is about the patient's name. About who she is. And about my name as chaplain: about who I am.

Another patient wanted to make sure I remembered his name. A black man, listed as "Hindu," who actually was a "Protestant"—and much more. "I never pass one church to get to another," he said. That was how he began sharing his beliefs: "God is love. Caring. Pitying. Forgiving. Strengthening. All of us need that. Whatever our religion or nationality or race." He was talking from experience. His wife left him with a three-and-a-half year-old son and an 18-month-old daughter whom he raised on his own. After he shared the story of his name, it was then time to offer prayer, that gave thanks for his god's merciful and affirming and empowering love for him and for all persons. For those for whom it has meaning, prayer can be a powerful way to say their name and reinforce their faith.

Three days later I unknowingly walked by the above patient on the unit while he was doing physical therapy. When I circled the unit again and approached, he stopped me. I looked at him and immediately recognized and spoke his full name. He said, "I don't want you to forget me." I replied, "I will never forget you, nor your powerful words about a loving god who cares for everyone." He then introduced me to his 50-year-old son, who was leading his father around the unit with one hand while pulling his father's IV machine with the other hand. I said, "So this is the son you raised from age three-and-a-half." "Yes," he replied. "While I was out winning the bread, he was home running the house." The patient then spoke words of praise about the one who was at his side all these years. Confused, I guessed, "Your son?" "God," he replied. And his son quickly added, "Me, too." A three-and-a-half year-old son, now a 50-year-old man, leading his 78-year-old father around the Unit. It is about love freely given and freely returned.

Remembering and saying patients' and family members' names help to create a common ground of humanness. I occasionally visited a young, critically ill, often unconscious, male Muslim patient in an intensive care unit. His mother stood vigil at his bedside. Early on she asked me to speak to her son, to give him a blessing. It was about saying his name, and the name and blessing upon him of their god, Allah. It was about the names held dear in the heart of a loving mother.

Many Christian patients respond very positively to prayers ending "in Jesus' name." So true the hymn: "How sweet the Name of Jesus sounds in a believer's ear!" Made even sweeter by the *sound* of the patient's own name.

Remembering and saying people's names is so important in pastoral care and in other relationships. I made it a point to transcend my negative perception of a white female hospital staff person's abrupt and angry demeanor and manner, for which she was known— especially by those of us who did not personally know her and were turned off by her unfriendly appearance. A key element in moving beyond my own guardedness toward her was remembering and saying her name—and taking the time to speak with and listen to her. In time, she began sharing conflicting religious beliefs and asking personal questions. There was also the sharing of a story or two. I began to enjoy seeing and sharing with her. I *grew* to like her.

In a recent conversation, she said that she stopped going to church years ago because she did not agree with certain beliefs held by her denomination, which evidently led her to ask me, "Can you tell by looking at people whether they are good or bad?" I replied, "I can tell by looking at people that they are human beings." She answered with a smile.

Pastoral care is about remembering and saying people's names—not just about praying for them in another's name. It is not about "God talk" but about listening and responding to what patients are saying and not saying. It is about affirming them not trying to "save" them. It is about them getting better not being better. It is about looking at people and seeing human beings.

6. "I want to get tight with him"

Upon entering 7 West, I was greeted by the Unit Secretary who said, "Rev. Alberts, the patient in Room 16A wants to talk to you." An example of the importance of a chaplain's visibility on patient floors meeting the need for immediate availability. As I headed for 16A, the patient's nurse approached and informed me, "The patient has cancer that's spread throughout his body. And, at his request, he was just made DNR (Do Not Resuscitate) and DNI (Do Not Intubate). He's just coming to terms with what they mean." I entered the 80-year-old black man's room, introduced myself and stated, "You wanted to see me." "Yes," he answered. "I want to get tight with him."

The word "tight" had a human ring. Impressed by his street language, I assumed whom he probably meant by "him," but wanted the patient to identify "him" in his own words. So, I asked, "You want to get tight with whom?" He replied, "With God. I'm a believer, but not a good Christian." "What is a good Christian?" I asked. "One who goes to church," he replied. That is what he was taught, like so many people. Being a "good Christian" is equated with attending church. The church salesmanship pitch of many a pastor and priest and their denominational leaders. The institution as an end in itself, rather than a means of affirming and enabling everyone's worth and rights—a contradiction of Jesus' teaching, "I came that they might have life, and have it more abundantly." (John 10:10, American Standard Version).

Around age 13, the patient thought about being really "tight with God" by becoming a minister—evidently influenced by his devout and caring 90-year-old grandmother. But he did not pursue this calling. "At that time [in Atlanta, Georgia and everywhere else]" he said, "there was segregation, and I didn't think I could get the education needed to become a minister." A commentary here is that, in his youth, he made "light" of his grandmother's urgings that he attend school. The ambition and hopes of a black youth "segregated" and suffocated. He made "light" of "segregated" education and

32

restricted opportunity that he believed led nowhere. Still, today he called himself a "jerk" for being a "jokester" in the face of his grandmother's pleadings for him to attend school. This grandson, who grew up with eight sisters, all now deceased, but with nephews and nieces who are nearby and visit him.

The cancer-riddled, bone-thin patient's story was occasionally and sharply interrupted by his intense struggle to cough up phlegm. "I'm so weak," he said, coughing. "Hit me on the back," which I did. "More. Harder!" He finally coughed up and spit out a glob in a container.

Being a "jerk" is part of growing up, I told him. "I was a jerk at times. Everyone has been." At different points during the visit, I told him that "God loves all of us very much—in church or out." That "God loves you very much." That "Jesus touched the lives of all kinds of people to reveal that God is 'tight' with everyone." He said that he believed his god loved him. But, in the face of death, it was about him being "*tight* with God."

The patient was receptive to my offer of prayer—so much so that he held my right hand very, very *tight* throughout the prayer, *and far beyond*—a prayer that affirmed him and his god's love for him. We had become "tight." I listened to his story, understood something of the struggle of an 80-year-old cancer-stricken black man growing up in a "segregated," and still white-controlled and favored society. A black man whose faith in an eternally loving god seemed to be reaffirmed. At the end of the visit, he held up his fist for me to tap with my fist, and, as I did, he repeated, "I feel much stronger now." "Good. You're a good man," I replied. It was about him being "tight" with another human being who represented that which is believed to be forever lovingly "tight" with everyone.

7. "Little things mean a lot"

It was toward the end of the day, and I was tired. Upon visiting the next patient, I asked if I could sit down. "Sure," he said. Then he reminded me why "little things mean a lot."

A 60-year-old white owner of a cranberry bog, the patient was sitting behind a metal table, with a pencil laying on a paper that had writing on it. He began, "I had this burning sensation in my chest, and thought it was from the medication I was taking for acid indigestion. But it persisted and got worse," he continued. "I finally went to my doctor. He told me how foolish I was, that I needed open heart surgery right away, and referred me to the hospital for surgery. Suddenly I went from indigestion to open heart surgery. And I'm wondering, 'How did that happen?'"

The patient then said, "Little things mean a lot." He explained: "I'm here, and I'm scared. I didn't know what to expect. They wheel me down to the operating room. And the doctors there are warmly greeting me, calling me by my name, asking how I'm doing, and joking with me-- as if I have nothing to worry about. They made me feel a lot better." He went on, "And I'm doing well. So, I've been thinking about writing a letter thanking them," and with that he held up the paper laying on the tray. I responded that such a letter would probably be very much appreciated by the doctors and the hospital.

There is more to his story. He said, "The doctors would come into my room and sit down and talk with me. They took the time to explain everything to me, and asked if I had questions, and answered them." His next words put flesh and blood on Boston Medical Center's mission statement ["Exceptional Care. Without Exception."]: *"For them, it was not routine"* (italics added)

The patient's words of appreciation for his doctors led me to repeat my assumption that they no doubt would be pleased to know of his appreciation of their care for him. He responded by verbalizing more determination to write such a letter. He said, "They took the time to sit down and listen to me, like you have done."

My tiredness is what initially led me to sit down in his room. I possibly still would have heard his story standing up. But sitting down more likely suggests to a patient that a pastoral care visit is not routine, and may invite more story telling by patients. Though pastoral care is about one's presence, not posture.

This patient reminded me of another case in which "little things mean a lot." The case involved an older Asian man who died, and his hospital room was filled with family and friends. A lay leader of his biblically-based church had assigned Scripture readings to certain persons present, and I was asked to offer a prayer. Hymns also were sung, as the patient had sung in the church choir, along with his wife. And the most inspiring moments came when the patient's wife and their adult daughters and sons stood at the foot of his bed and sang family songs to him in their native language. Then, his wife, whose voice was as mellow as Kitty Kallens's, who recorded the following song, sang to him,

Blow me a kiss across the room
Say I look nice when I'm not
Touch my hair as you pass my chair
Little things mean a lot.

Give me your arm as we cross the street
Call me at six on the dot
A line a day when you're far away
Little things mean a lot.

Don't have to buy me diamonds or pearls
Champagne, sables or such
I never cared much for diamonds and pearls
'Cause honestly, honey, they just cost money.

Give me your hand when I've lost my way
Give me your shoulder to cry on
Whether the day is bright or gray
Give me your heart to rely on.

Send me the warmth of a secret smile
To show me you haven't forgot
For always and ever, now and forever
Little things mean a lot.

(Words and music by Edith Lindeman and Carl Stutz)

Chaplaincy is about discovering the little things that mean a lot to patients and their loved ones.

8. "You could have written my name on a blackboard, and I wouldn't have known it"

The Jehovah's Witness patient was not trying to get me to subscribe to his denomination's magazine, *The Watchtower*. Nor trying to convert me to his religion. He was like other Jehovah's Witness patients, whose humanness often shows up once their religion is affirmed with, "May the blessings of Jehovah be upon you." This Jehovah's Witness patient told me his story, sharing a message that has implications for any religion.

An 83-year-old black man, in an intensive care unit, suffering a stroke, the patient engaged me as soon as I introduced myself and answered his questions about my chaplaincy and the kinds of patients I visit. "I was a Methodist until 30 years ago," he began. "I listened to ministers preach from the Bible, and believed what they said. I didn't know anything different. I was uneducated. I couldn't even read or write."

He continued, "Then this Jehovah's Witness came to my door. He taught me how to read and write. He came to my home every week," the patient went on. "And he used the Bible, giving me passages to read, which we would go over. It took a long while, but in time I began to read and understand the Bible for myself."

The patient ended, "You could have written my name on a blackboard, and I wouldn't have known it. *But I know it now.* And the man who taught me couldn't read or write at one time himself."

Religion is about teaching people how to read and write their own name—and learn for themselves. It is also about the messenger becoming the message.

Chaplaincy is about helping people tell the story of *their name*.

9. "You gave me my humanity"

I entered a patient's room by mistake, and left with a surprising message. A 64-year-old white man had told me the day before that he was not affiliated with a religion. He happened to have been moved to the room that had been occupied by a patient I intended to visit. I was surprised to see him again. When patients say they are unaffiliated, I wish them a good day and good progress in their treatment. I have no desire to market religion—and an aversion to conversion, as the desire to convert people to one's own religious belief violates their right to be who they are. I take my cue from patients. If they want to interact, they let me know in different ways, and I respond. Evidently, the coincidence of seeing this patient again helped to lead him and me to engage in an extended conversation, with him doing much of the talking and I the listening.

The patient began to tell his story. "I believe in God," he said. "I see God in what I call ordinary miracles, not in big ones." A botanist by hobby, he stated, "I can take one plant and breed it with another and make a third species of plant. But I cannot create the original plant that I used. The original is God's doing."

"Ordinary miracles and not big ones," I said. "Yes," the patient replied.

He continued. "I believe in God but not in organized religion." He then gave the example of Mormon youths coming to his home to convert him to their religion. He asked them, "Do you believe that yours is the one true religion?" They said, "Yes." That, he said is what turns him off about religion.

The patient was just getting warmed up. "Picture the world as a puzzle, and each of the religions a piece of the puzzle. If I had the power and wanted to make the world be at war against itself, I would tell each group that its religion was the true one. All the groups," he continued, "would be trying to convert each other and fighting would ensue. And the pieces of the puzzle could not be put together to reunite the world."

The patient then stated, "Power corrupts." He then quoted the English historian, Lord Acton, who said, "Power tends to corrupt, and absolute power corrupts absolutely." The patient said that organized Christianity, Catholic and Protestant, "is the anti-Christ." Their aim, he believes, is to gain power over people, not empower them. It is not about "love your neighbor as yourself" as Jesus taught, but about which has the biggest miracle and thus the biggest piece of "the puzzle."

The patient then went to the heart of his story. He retired early from a professional position, and began tutoring children in English and Math. He said, "I have no children of my own, so my aim was to help other children to learn and obtain knowledge." He said it was a challenging task, and involved teaching lessons for ten minutes, then playing Scrabble or Chinese Checkers with the children for a period of time, then back to the lessons. He discovered that this technique enabled the children to better grasp and integrate material.

One of the students he tutored grew up and became a state representative. He went to his former student's election victory party. He jokingly told the state representative that he wanted to look at his victory speech to see the influence of his tutoring years ago. He said, "The state representative replied, 'You gave me my humanity.'" The patient then choked up, and added, "At that moment the world stood still for me. His words led me to feel that I could have died right then and life would have been fulfilled for me."

Pastoral care is about enabling patients to tell their stories, the sharing of which affirms and empowers the teller and often provides wisdom for the listener.

10. A Prayer and A Paper

If one patient had his way, a hospital would be like a hotel, with the daily paper placed next to every patient's room each morning.

He was an often-admitted, 48-year-old, diabetic, black patient whom I first met some sixteen years ago. We soon discovered that we had a mutually revered friend in common. A black colleague, who has made a tremendous contribution to my understanding of racial issues and to my research and published writings about these and other social justice concerns. The very same colleague whom the patient, years ago, helped to become dean of a local university's School of Public and Community Service. He and other students had successfully advocated for my colleague's appointment as dean. Having such a mutually valued friend provided initial bonding for a long-term pastoral care relationship, which early on became characterized by a prayer and a paper.

Each time I entered his room, the patient would be watching a news program on television or reading a morning paper—both of which, along with his having worked for the federal government, fed his deep interest in political issues and current events. Thus news events became part of our conversations. Early on, he invited me to assist his daily ritual-- "Rev. Alberts, the woman who usually gets my papers is not here today. Could you get them for me? *The Boston Globe* and *The Boston Herald*." "Sure," I replied. His avid interest in the news is seen in his reading *both* papers—and any other if they were not available.

From that time on, I made sure he had his daily papers. For I, too, believe a hospital should be like a hotel in this regard. I also believe that whatever engages and lifts an individual's spirit is sacred, whether it be the pages of *The Bible* or *The Globe* and *The Herald*.

In time, he would ask for me upon each of his admissions. "Hey, Rev. Alberts, the patient in room 16A would like to see you," one or another nurse or unit secretary would say.

Once, as I entered his room, he was being treated by his doctor.

As I turned back toward the door, he saw me and said, "Rev. Alberts, come in. Come in." "I don't want to interrupt your doctor," I replied. "Rev. Alberts needs to come in," he ordered his doctor. The doctor happily invited me in.

On another occasion, when I brought him the morning papers, he began browsing through one, slowing skimming each page with a smile, as I sat on a chair at the foot of his bed. He seemed to forget I was there. Shortly, as if reminding himself of my presence, he said, "Ah, Rev. Alberts, could you offer a prayer?"

Prayer was important to this man, and evidently an ongoing source of affirmation and empowerment throughout his coping with life-threatening illnesses. During these 16 years, he had a leg amputated, underwent major open heart surgery, and spent time daily in the dialysis unit—with occasional critical episodes at home (he lived alone) leading him to be rushed by ambulance to the hospital.

The patient's requests for prayer usually preceded his requests for the daily papers. On a memorable occasion, I entered his room when he was sitting in a chair and cleaning up in the bathroom, with the door partly open. "I'm in here, Rev. Alberts," he called out. He asked if I could get him the papers, and then said, "But first, would you offer a prayer?"—and then extended his hand through the bathroom door for me to hold.

Later on, during these many years, the patient joined a local Baptist church, to which his aunt belonged. A devoted and loving pastoral care volunteer, who worked with me visiting patients for years, and who also was a member of that church, helped him to make the congregation his church family. He invited me to join with the pastoral care volunteer in sponsoring him at the church's membership ceremony, which I gladly did. The Baptist church provided him with real family and support that had been missing in his life.

Sadly, the patient died in July 2010 at age 64. This story is a tribute to him.

Pastoral care is about providing a prayer -- and a paper.

11. "I should have done more for him"

She was one of three daughters and numerous nieces and nephews, who were at their dying 72-year-old white Catholic father's and grandfather's bedside. The hospital's Catholic chaplain was on retreat, and the patient had received the Anointing of the Sick; but the family still wanted a chaplain to offer a prayer for their dying loved one. I responded to the request, and offered the prayer, for which not only the family but the patient thanked me. Two days later the patient died, and I was paged again to his bedside. Only one family member had remained: the oldest daughter, who greeted me with a universal feeling of regret: "I should have done more for him."

This oldest daughter may have been the last to leave her dead father's bedside because of a feeling of guilt that she had not been there enough for him. "What do you mean, you should have done more for him?" I asked. "He's been ill for seven months, and I've only seen him a couple times a week. I should have seen him more." She continued. "I didn't realize he was going to die. And I have other concerns."

"What other concerns do you have?" I asked. "I have a seven-year-old son to take care of," she said. I recalled my first visit, and how she and her sisters surrounded their father, and *touched* him with their love—stroking his brow and telling him that they were all there and loved him very much. I shared with her my perception of that initial visit. I then said, "Your father knows that you love him. You and your sisters surrounded him with your love." I then told her that she should not play god with herself that she could not have known he would die in seven months. "And you had your son to care for as well."

How many fathers, had they known they were going to die, would have done more for their daughters? And for others? *Self-love is walking in ones own shoes with the same understanding that one would afford others.*

This lingering daughter then spoke of her son: "Tommy wanted to come and visit his grandpa, and not stay at home or in the visitors' room here. So, I brought him in the other day, and dad's face lighted up. 'Oh, it's Tommy!' And a big smile crossed his face." I said what she already knew: "That is a loving way for Tommy to remember his grandfather."

I offered a prayer affirming the preciousness of the love that this daughter and her father have for each other. Which was followed by my hugging her, and her thanking me.

The daughter then shared with me a framed picture, hanging from her neck, of her son, in a Pee Wee league baseball uniform and holding a bat—and hanging next to it on another chain was a crucifix. "Here's a picture of my son in his baseball uniform," she said with a proud smile. She then added, broadening her smile, "And I'm the coach of his baseball team." "That's wonderful!" I exclaimed.

A picture of her son and a cross hanging together. The one a symbol of continuing love that delights in, nourishes life, and passes it on. The other also a symbol, of unconditional love that understands and forgives and affirms and frees one to continue passing life on.

12. The Rainbow Itself Is the Pot of Gold

A hospital especially reveals the diversity and connectedness of human beings, their individuality and commonality, their uniqueness and oneness. Patients and their families represent the various Christian denominations and other religions, races, nationalities, cultures, political ideologies and sexual orientations that make up the human community—ecumenical, interfaith, inter-human. Life unfolds itself in various colors, revealing that the rainbow itself is the pot of gold. That any creator of life is a god of diversity, not uniformity. A hospital especially also reveals not only humanity's diversity but its commonality as well. Illness confronts all people with their mortality and hence their vulnerability, their humanness—their oneness and connectedness with each other.

Like the 75-year-old white male patient, unaffiliated with a religion, who expressed a powerful meaning of thanksgiving for life itself. His lengthy hospitalization with a life-threatening illness led me to say, "I assume that being confined like this for a long time would lead you to think about what is most important to you." He replied, "I don't know what isn't important any more." He speaks for and to all of us. When we are confronted with our mortality, we stop taking life for granted and become deeply thankful for the life we are granted.

Another patient provides an inspiring example of self-determination. A black Protestant woman in her 40's, she said, "My mother always told me, 'You have two hands and legs and a head; use them; you're as good as anyone else.'"

A third patient expresses an inclusive worldview. When I noted that he was listed as "Hindu," the 70-year-old man replied, "I'm everything. Why limit me to a definition? The East and the West are confinements," he continued. "The eagle soars throughout the heavens—not just in one direction or another."

This patient reveals our common human tendency: we often define people to confine them. It is better to label poison, not people; illnesses, not ideas; drugs, not dreams. Too often, right and wrong get lost in "left" and "right." We honor people by respecting their differences, by experiencing their reality, not interpreting it. By individualizing among people, not stereotyping them.

A fourth person affirmed the precious humanness of his just deceased 84-year-old black Baptist father, in a touching, spontaneous eulogy at the foot of his father's hospital bed. "Dad, you held on until the rest of the family could get here to say good-by to you. You were always like that," the son went on, "always caring about others. You've done so much in your life. We're so proud of you. You've been everywhere, and done everything—and made a few things up along the way," he added with a tearful smile. "Not that you needed to." Then, with tears in his eyes, the son sat down next to his father.

A final patient, a white 65-year-old Christian woman, had undergone two unexpected surgeries, and when finally ready, and eager, to be discharged, developed an infection which continued to hospitalize and depress her. "I had had it," she said. "I just stopped trying, stopped fighting to get better. I gave in and just left it in God's hands. I had given up," she continued. "But later, when I heard my roommate start to hum 'Love lifted me,' my body surged upward; and then she began to sing the words." Untold numbers of hospital patient roommates are wonderful pastoral care givers.

A hospital is a unique crossroads of humanity. It entertains the varieties of religious and human experience—and calls forth the tremendous related wisdom of all kinds of patients and their families.

Chaplaincy is about honoring patients and their families in calling them by their own names.

13. "Jesus and I travel light"

Hospital patients reveal the power-- and humanness-- of belief in a personal god.

A 42-year-old black Baptist woman demonstrates the empowerment of belief in her god. Her face grimacing and voice groaning in pain, she told her story: "I have lupus and my kidneys shut down." Moaning in painful interruptions, she continued, "I'm going to tell this, and the devil isn't going to stop me. God is seeing me through this pain." With considerable effort, she talked about her illnesses and her family. And after welcoming a prayer, she said, "God bless you," and added, "God sent you." She requested that I visit her again.

She was moved to an intensive care unit, where I next saw her. Although intubated, she was very much awake and oriented. When I asked if she were still in pain, she nodded, then wrote on a pad, "God is dealing with it!" When I asked if she would like me to offer a prayer, she scribbled, "Yes. Yes. Yes." Having no shield to protect her from the slings and arrows of her pain, she evidently wrapped herself in the biblical breastplate of her god's love for and protection of her.

The power of belief in one's god is seen in the surprising response of a 70-year-old black Protestant patient. Since she looked familiar, I asked if we had met before. She replied, "Yes," then said, "I still remember when you visited me 8 years ago. I was near death, and you prayed for me, and lifted my spirits. I'll never forget that." She reveals that it is not just what a chaplain's prayer may bring to a patient, but what a patient's belief in her god may bring to a chaplain's prayer.

The human need for a relationship that is accepting and supportive is seen in the testimony of a 42-year-old white United Church of Christ woman. When I asked if she were affiliated with a church, she said, "No. Just Jesus. Jesus and I travel light." "You and Jesus: a good combination," I said. "Yes," she answered. "He's been with me all the way." She probably could have named people close to her who have not been with her all the way. That is what an ideal accepting and empowering human relationship is about: with an available, non-judgmental, trustworthy, challenging person in whom one can confide. A relationship that lightens rather than increases one's burdens.

Certain religious institutions do not meet people's human need to "travel light," i.e., to be able to safely bare themselves to make life more bearable. When I asked a 55-year-old white woman patient if she were affiliated with a church, she replied, "No. I've been a bad girl." Her church attendance-conditioned conscience was echoed by a 70-year-old white male Protestant patient who answered the same question with, "No, I'm one of those bad boys."

It should not be about equating being "good" or "bad" with church attendance. It should be about accepting and supportive relationships that create a sanctuary of honesty, thereby better enabling people to appreciate and make room for the humanness and rights of others.

Many patients find in their god the accessibility, acceptance, affirmation and empowerment that are often lacking in their human relationships. Like the 27-year old adopted black daughter of a father who had just died, and whose adoptive mother died two years ago. When I asked if she had someone to talk to, she replied, "God." "Any friends?" I continued. "No," she replied. "People suck. You can't count on them. They suck. Sorry for my language. But that is just the way it is."

The gospel hymn expresses well the interpersonal human need of this adopted daughter and many other individuals:

I come to the garden alone
While the dew is still on the roses
And the voice I hear falling on my ear
The Son of God discloses.

And He walks with me, and He talks with me.
And He tells me I am His own;
And the joy we share as we tarry there,
None other has ever known.
(IN THE GARDEN, Words & Music: C. Austin Miles)

While one's heavenly god is believed to be superhuman, such a belief is often grounded in unmet human need. Chaplaincy is about embodying in the flesh a patient's need of trust, acceptance and affirmation.

47

14. "In the zone"

The 52-year-old black Protestant hospital patient was about to tell and show me, as a chaplain, what it means to be "in the zone." It was not about spirituality but about sports. Not about praying but about playing. It was not about divinity but about a diamond, on which he sparkled-- a baseball diamond. "The zone" he invited me into was far more therapeutic than any theological discussion.

Sitting slouched and limp in a chair next to his bed after serious open-heart surgery, he came alive during my visit when our conversation, for some reason, turned to Major League baseball. "I could make the Majors today if I were 19," he said, and continued, "I played little league baseball and in the Connie Mack league. But you had to go to college to get in the majors."

When I asked the position he played, he said, "Centerfield. I was fast. I could catch a ball hit anywhere. You go get 'em, man," he added, his body moving forward, his arms outstretched, and his big hands opening and closing as if catching a fly ball. "I was in the zone," he said, "completely focused on the game." I could picture him roaming centerfield, and the lightening speed with which he would run after a fly ball.

He was just getting warmed up. "My two friends played in the outfield too. We played in South Chicago, and our team tore up the league," he said, putting his hands together and moving them forward as if swinging a bat at a ball. "And I could run those bases," he went on, his animated body going through the motions of playing the game, and repeatedly saying, "I was in the zone."

Having played sandlot baseball myself and followed the game over the years, I invited him into my "zone," sharing with him my pitching a no-hitter just before entering the Navy in 1944 at age 17. And trying out with the Pittsburgh Pirates at age 25, and finally being allowed to pitch in the 9th inning-- to the last batter, who popped out on my third pitch. So, with a heavy heart, I drove back to the student church I was serving, and continued my seminary education.

There was the sharing together of two similar sacred "zones." And the mutual recalling of some of baseball's greats, like Ernie Banks of the Chicago Cubs, and Mickey Mantle of the New York Yankees, and New York Giants centerfielder Willie Mays, and Bob Gibson of the St. Louis Cardinals, and Ted Williams of the Boston Red Sox.

Our conversation lasted for "nine innings." Upon leaving, I thanked him for sharing. He replied, "Thank you for sharing *too*." Then he said, "It is something we will never forget." I replied, "I will remember it my whole life." There was no need for a benediction. We were both blessed in sharing being "in the zone."

15. "What do you tell someone who is going to die?"

She is a 47-year-old white patient, diagnosed with a large growth which she decided not to treat with chemotherapy. The treatment would prolong her life temporarily, but at a cost that she was unwilling to endure. Thus her question to me was, "What do you tell someone who is going to die?"

A member of the Unity Christian faith, her question apparently was not motivated by a fear of dying and going to hell. She believes in the inherent goodness and unconditional love of her god, and thus in the inherent goodness of people, who are made in such a god's image. Here, Jesus serves not as a personal savior but as a living embodiment and example of the divine essence, which a spiritually mindful person may attain. And prayer and meditation are the connection to a god who brings out and enlarges one's own innate goodness and love. And the bottom line is honoring and enabling the inherent humanness and goodness and rights of others.

"What do you tell someone who is going to die?" That is a very difficult question. I'm not sure what I would tell myself if dying were imminent for me. So my initial answer to her was theological—and heartfelt at best.

I shared with her my belief in a universally loving god. A god whose creative spirit is seen in birth and growth and renewal. I also said that such a creative universal spirit reveals that every life is equally precious and worthy. Aware that what she thought about her own dying was key, I then turned the question around: "What are your concerns about dying?"

The patient was concerned about her legacy, and about not having time to finish what she wanted to accomplish. She is a specialist in emerging technologies and knowledge management, a photographer, and a writer of non-denominational, spiritually mindful newspaper columns. I suggested that she might list her priorities, and seek to complete them as she is able—a suggestion she liked, but soon realized she was unable to pursue because of the toll her medication took on her energy and alertness. She was not without support. Her minister and members of her church visited her. And she and her "Momma Bear" older sister transcended long-standing differences when the former visited her; and "it was good," the patient said.

Earlier on, she requested a prayer, which I offered. She continued to hold my hand tightly long after the prayer—revealing her need for something, and someone, to hold on to.

But it was the honest sharing of myself that, I believe, was my most helpful way of affirming her innate worth—and legacy as a human being. During my second visit, her curiosity about me led her to ask personal questions I've rarely encountered from patients. "Why did you enter the ministry?" I replied, "To impress my girlfriend at the time, who was very religious." The patient smiled. I think I suddenly became real to her. I also think she realized that my honesty revealed that she had suddenly become real to me. She perceptively said, "If it were not real, you wouldn't have stayed in it." She then asked, "How long have you been a minister?" I replied, "Sixty-one years." She then asked, "Do you like it more now?" "I like it more in the last 30-some years. I like who I am and what I do. I believe everyone is equally precious." She smiled again.

Honesty is a powerful way of affirming a patient's own inherent worth and goodness. The empowerment of honesty—the affirmation of trust and inherent worth bequeathed from one person to another.

51

16. When You Start Off on the Wrong Foot

When you start off on the wrong foot, back up and start over. I took this advice from myself.

A 63-year-old black Protestant woman patient was dying on another campus, and when I responded to the initial page, not all of the family was there. When all of the family arrived, the nurse paged me again, and I returned to the patient's room. The daughter, for whom other family members were waiting, had just arrived in her mother's room with a friend. When we met, she said that two of her sisters, whom I saw on my initial visit, had gone to the cafeteria for breakfast. She also stated that she and her friend were "going out for a smoke." With it being Sunday and approaching noon, I said to the daughter, "I have a short ecumenical service that I lead at 12 o'clock, and I will return as soon as it's over." The daughter looked at me with a blank stare and did not respond. Her silence led me to ask, "Do you understand what I am saying?" She replied, "I understand you perfectly."

The daughter's words stayed with me. I had no problem with the two daughters going to the cafeteria for breakfast. And I was a chain-smoker for years myself, until I quit "cold turkey." And I have a lasting appreciation of the need "for a cigarette." Still, was I annoyed at making a second trip to the patient's room on the other campus, only to be told by the later arriving daughter that she and her friend were "going out for a smoke?"

Did this daughter hear me "perfectly"-- a white male chaplain possibly talking down to a black woman in my asking if she understood my plain English? Or, was she having difficulty getting her mind around a white male chaplain suddenly appearing to provide pastoral care for her black family? With these speculations in mind, I backed up and started over. I was aware that people have needs that don't, nor should not have to, fit into my schedule. *In due time* is determined by the realities and priorities of patients and their loved ones.

A big loving and grieving family, consisting of five daughters and a son and grandson and other relatives and friends, surrounded the intubated and sedated patient. The daughter, who gave me pause, stood next to her mother's bed, wiping her brow and telling her, "We're all here, mother. We love you so much. You've done everything for us." Her testimony was followed by similarly loving words of other family members, which led me to say, "You are a very loving family." The daughter who first spoke replied, "It's because of her." "Yes," I said, "she is the *one* who passed her love on to all of you. Your love for her and for each other is very precious." I seek to make such hopefully timely brief comments in an attempt to express the meaningful realities of and thus bring comfort to grieving loved ones.

This is a religious family. Three of the daughters stood at the foot of their mother's bed and softly and in harmony sang to her Andrae Crouch's gospel song:

Soon and very soon,
We are going to see the King!
Soon and very soon,
We are going to see the King,
Halle-lu-jah! Hallelujah!

No more crying there,
We are going to see the King!
No more crying there,
We are going to see the King!

No more dying there,
We are going to see the King!
No more dying there,
We are going to see the King!

Halle-lu-jah! Halle-lu-jah!

We all joined hands around this loving mother and grandmother and friend, and I offered a prayer that held up their love for her and for one another, and their god's love for her and for providing "no more crying [nor] dying there."

There was another prayer offered, by a Christian woman minister and close friend of the patient and her family. A prayer that everyone heard through the speaker of a cell phone, as the prayer-giver was unable to be present. Her prayer was filled with love and wisdom: "Father God, bless this loving family. Father God, whatever your will is. If you take their dear one to yourself, help them to accept it and to love each other all the more in this time of their grief . . ." The prayer-giver's daughter was present. I later expressed to her my appreciation of her mother's beautifully supportive prayer, and asked that she convey my appreciation to her mother.

There was a moment of humor. At one point, when Dale, the white male nurse, entered the room, the daughter positioned beside the patient said, "Dale, ever time you enter the room my mother's eyes light up, and she perks up. She has a thing for you." Everybody laughed, including Dale who said, "I do the best I can."

As the end drew near, the patient's grandson stood outside her room, crying and repeating, "I don't want her to leave." He plans to attend a technical school because, he said, "I'm not good with books." His aunts told him that they would now help him carry out his plans. At one point, I told him that, as he knew, his grandmother would want him to attend technical school and make the best of his life. He nodded knowingly.

As life ebbed from the patient during this hour-and-a-half, the daughter standing next to her, sensing her mother had just died, screamed helplessly, "Someone help my mother!" She then ran from the room and fell just outside the doorway, where two other staff persons and I picked her up; and she then returned to the room. A few minutes later she asked Dale to cut off a piece of her mother's hair, which he did and put in a small cellophane container for her. The various human ways in which we remember and resurrect our loved ones.

Love is not just about a stiff upper lip, but about a woundable human heart. The daughter I met in the beginning turned into who she was before my eyes: a strong and vulnerable loving daughter and sister and aunt. At the end, I gave her a firm, sympathetic hug, which she returned in kind.

The role of Dale, the nurse, was especially important to the daughters and son and other family members. As they left the room, each spontaneously gave him a special hug and said, "Thank you for taking care of our mother."

Chaplaincy is about both feet planted responsively amidst the realities and strengths and needs of patients and their loved ones.

17. "Pray that I win the lottery"

A 54-year-old black patient, who identified herself as "just a Christian," expressed a very human need and wish when I asked if she would like me to offer a prayer. "Yes, sir," she responded, raising both hands, "and pray that I win the lottery." So I prayed, "God of love, you heard Rachel Henry. If possible, may she win the lottery. You know we all need money," I continued. "We thank you for loving us whether we have money or not, and for being with us in our good times and bad. And we thank you for all that blesses and nourishes and renews Rachel Henry."

While a god of luck soon runs out on people, in our non-discriminatory cause and effect world, a god who plays favorites also lets people down. A classic example is the family of a 64-year-old white evangelical Christian patient, whose members constantly prayed that their mother and wife would live, in spite of the oft-repeated medical reality that she was dying. And scientific technology was actually keeping her alive, and not the family's prayers as the members needed to believe. And, ironically, the patient was actually undergoing more suffering by the family's prolonging of her dying in keeping her on an intubator—so that she could stay alive long enough for their god to answer their prayers with a miracle. This situation became intolerable for certain nurses who protested the patient's continued suffering by refusing to continue caring for her.

Tragically, the family's evident literal belief in the Bible led them to take Jesus at his recorded word: "And whatever you ask in prayer, you will receive if you have faith." (Matthew 21: 22) Sadly, the onus appeared to be on them to have *enough* "faith," and not on their god. Or on their evangelistic teachers, whose apparent dumbing down of their deity accommodated the biblical teachers' own ignorance and assumed authority and power-seeking and their followers' apparent need for certainty of belief.

The patient died, possibly leaving the devoted family in a spiritual Catch-22 of anger and guilt and worsened depression. The family seems to have been left hanging by a reality-denying god, who is believed to favor and award only those who shower him with prayer. The medical staff and I, as hospital chaplain, continued, with some difficulty, to support the family members throughout their painful vigilant struggle to keep their loved one alive.

Prayer reveals much about people and about the god to whom they pray. It is very natural—and human—for people of faith, and others as well, to seek divine help when they are struggling with their finances or their finitude in life's foxholes. But the act of prayer to a personal god is based on the belief that prayer is needed for one's god to respond. Furthermore, the act of such prayer is based on the assumption or hope that one's god will favor the one who prays. Prayer, therefore, reveals the subtlety and pervasiveness of belief in a god who favors one person over another—and, sadly, one nation ("God bless America") over another.

A 71-year-old white male Jewish patient, who is agnostic, revealed how religious belief can determine perception. When I asked his religion, which was unknown, he began by toying with me: "I'm an atheist, thank God," he responded, smiling. Then he said, "For some people, seeing is believing. For other people, believing is seeing."

Prayer is about one's god, and more. "Keep me in your prayers," is an individual's way of asking to be thought of and cared for, especially in his or her time of need. Prayer is a way of communicating that one is *standing by* a person who is, in the words of the gospel song, "standing in the need of prayer." For chaplains, prayer is a powerful way of affirming a patient, by calling forth divine Love that is unconditional and constant and universal.

How kind and generous and compassionate and forgiving, yes, how just and inclusive and loving—one's god is *towards oneself and others* depends greatly on one's own inner emotional makeup and cultural conditioning.

Religion should help people perceive and deal with reality-- and transform it with acts of compassion and justice and love-- not short cut or deny it. Equally important, rather than preferring one person or group over another, religion should help people to love their neighbor as themselves, as Jesus and other great spiritual leaders have taught. For it is from people's own integrated self-awareness and – self-affirmation that flow understanding and caring of neighbors near and far.

18. The Various Ways in Which the Human Spirit Moves Its Wonders to Perform

Spirituality reveals not only the infiniteness of divinity but the infinite varieties of humanity. "God moves in a mysterious way His wonders to perform," begins the faith-filled hymn of English poet William Cowper. While "God" is believed to "move in mysterious ways," hospital patients reveal the many and various ways in which the human spirit moves to perform its faith-inspired wonders.

The apparent empowering personal nature of spirituality is seen in the words of a 72-year-old black female Baptist patient, who has been blind and also suffering from a chronic illness for 40 years. She said that her repeated prayer is, "God, I'm sick and thank You anyhow. You've helped me through it for 40 years, and given me a loving husband and two wonderful children. I praise You," she continued "not just for the good times but for the bad times too, which You led me through." She was not thanking her god for curing her blindness but for *seeing* her through it – though she may well have prayed often for a miracle early on.

In the face of illness, injury, and death, many hospital patients and their families and friends find comfort and empowerment in the words, "Thank you, Jesus." Which they often spontaneously utter during my prayers for them. "Thank you, Jesus-- not for what has befallen them but for whom they believe is sustaining them in love.

The belief that one is loved is such a powerful transforming emotion. It can alleviate guilt, give peace of mind, inner strength, and connectedness. It can turn an individual around, lead one to be "born again," to become sober, clean, responsible, focused, creative.

Like the 60-year-old Latino evangelical man, who suddenly stopped abusing his body with alcohol and cigarettes when he discovered that someone else loved it and him—and revealed it was a temple of spirituality. That someone, he came to believe, through the caring of other persons, was Jesus, whom he accepted as his savior.

The amazing grace characterizing that acceptance not only helped to save him from years of self-abuse, but also inspired him to write religious songs and sing them for others in churches and on radio programs. Such transforming grace is also found in the love of one person for another.

While spirituality is personal and usually perceived as heaven sent, it also moves in horizontal ways its wonders to perform. Spirituality has a "human touch," and may be much more down to earth than is realized or understood—or appreciated. It may be impossible to know where an individual's emotional and physical make-ups end and spirituality begins.

For example, an attractive, older, wise and caring black female pastoral care volunteer and I visited a very sick-appearing, listless, prone black male patient in his 60's. As she stood next to his bedside and engaged him in conversation, his body began to stir. Their exchanges grew more spontaneous, personal, familiar, and even light-hearted joshing-- leading him to rise up in his bed, his body animated, his full smile reflecting an uplifted spirit. Her presence and their exchanges seemed to have not only made his day but his hospital stay. She had paid attention to him. And her ensuing prayer appeared to be anti-climatic. He had already caught the "spirit." Was it agape or eros? Or both?

While spirituality is believed to be personal and to come from above, its natural home is in interpersonal relationships. Recently, for example, the sister of a white female patient in her 80's said, after my prayer, "Your cheerfulness is a mark that Christ is within you."

On another occasion, an unmarried 42-year-old white female patient, whose baby was refused baptism at one church, said that she joined another church. Why? Because the minister invited anyone to question him about anything, which evidently encouraged her to be herself. And most important to her, the members of that church were accepting of and cared for her as a person. She had found a spiritual *home*.

A 35-year-old white Jewish female patient also stressed the integral connection between belief and behavior. When she identified her religion as Jewish, I said, "My daughter-in-law is Jewish." She replied, "I hope she is a good person."

Spirituality is deeply personal. It may be defined by but not confined to creed or ritual. It may be theologized but not monopolized. It may be entertained but not institutionalized. And where there is love, spirituality knows no barriers or borders to human community.

19. Out of the Mouth of Babes... and Older People

She is a 76-year-old black Baptist patient who fooled me. She did not possess grammatical nor theological refinement, but any seminary or political science class would benefit from her down-to-earth wisdom. As I entered her room, she was watching a television newscast of the ash billowing out of a volcano in Iceland and blackening the skies, and grounding airplanes to and from Europe. After introducing myself, I noted her eyes fixed on the television screen and asked, "What do you make of that?" She replied, "The world's collapsing." I asked what she meant by "collapsing," assuming she probably would paint a religiously-inspired doomsday-darkening-skies-picture of the end of the world. Instead, she revealed the wisdom of an ethicist and of a truly democratically-motivated diplomat.

"What do I mean by the world's collapsing?" she replied. "People aren't getting along. It's like, I'm *this one* and you're *that one*," which she emphasized by jerking her body first to the right and then to the left. "The world needs to become one."

She continued: "Why should I hate someone I don't know? If I get to know them, I may like them. And if I don't," she emphasized, "I can still be civil. I don't need to hate them."

Think of all the people being terrorized and killed and maimed and *radicalized* in unnecessary wars based on, "We're *this one* and you're *that one*." Think of all the people being oppressed by discriminatory immigration laws that tell them, "You're *that one*." Think of the patient, and all the other people of color like her, being told, "We're *this one* and you're *that one*," in America's continuing white-controlled hierarchy of access to economic and political power. Think of all the gay and lesbian and bisexual and transgender people still stereotyped and marginalized with, "We're *this one* and you're *that one*." Think of all the people who would benefit from foreign and domestic—and mainstream media editorial—policies based on the belief that "the world needs to become one"—to prevent it from "collapsing."

Out of the mouth of babes—and of older persons—comes much wisdom.

20. Caring Is About Timing—and Embracing the Unexpected

A puzzled-looking white man in his '40s' was still standing near an intersection of the hospital's hallways when I walked by a second time. He stopped me with, "Could you help me? We were told to wait in the visitor's room," he said, "and they'd come and get us in 20 minutes, before my sister's surgery. And it's been 45 minutes. We're worried about how she's doing." At that point, two women walked up and stood beside him, one the patient's sister and the other her cousin. Heading for the floors to begin a day of scheduled patient visits, I could have encouraged them to continue waiting for staff to come and take them to the patient. Hospital staff are quite conscientious, and a delay may be normal. But their anxiety led me, after introducing myself, to tell them to return to the visitor's room, and I would check on their family member, who, her brother had informed me, was Catholic.

An intensive care unit secretary assisted by responding to my question about the patient's status regarding her surgery, saying she was still in pre-op, and was scheduled to have a tumor removed from her ovaries. I then went to pre-op and found the patient, who was being prepared for the surgery. Upon explaining my mission, a nurse said that the patients' family could "come in now."

I returned to the family members, who now included the patient's daughter, and took them to the pre-op room where they were happily reunited with and surrounded the patient. I offered the patient a verbal blessing, and said that I would inform the Catholic chaplain of her presence when he arrived later in the morning. As I was about to leave, the patient's sister asked, "Would you say a prayer for my sister?" My prayer gave thanks for this family's love for each other, for the doctors' and nurses' commitment to the patient's well-being, for her god's love for her, and for all that affirms and nourishes and renews her. When I ended, the patient sighed audibly, and tears filled her eyes, and her family thanked me. Just as the patient's family felt suspended, not knowing where and how she was, she, too, felt suspended not knowing where they were, at this critical time of her need for their support.

The deep sigh and watery eyes and look of relief on this patient's face showed me the importance of being able to interrupt a planned schedule and respond to unexpected human need. What may appear to be a delay may prove to be very timely.

On another occasion, timing was not dependent on a chance contact. A 64-year-old black Baptist patient requested a chaplain to visit her. As soon as I arrived, she began a very needed sharing of what was uppermost on her mind. "My husband died seven months ago, and he had been a patient here, on various floors, where I'd visit him. He was also in another hospital, and in rehab," she went on, "for an amputation and then a stroke." She continued her story, "I prayed and prayed that he would come home before he died. I even bought a wheelchair for that day. And," she ended, "he came home for one day. One day! And then back to the hospital where he died."

What began as a matter-of-fact story became filled with emotion toward the end. "Your being here, where your husband also was a patient, reminds you of him very much," I said. "Yes," she replied, and then broke down and sobbed. She needed to tell someone, at this time, the story of her love for and loss of her husband, which her own hospitalization acutely brought to the fore. She may or may not have been able to express such grieving since he died. But, in the hospital, it yearned for expression and to be heard. I offered a prayer that held up, before her god, the preciousness of the love she and her husband shared—an unending love.

Chaplaincy, like any meaningful relationship, is about taking the time to respond to human need. Caring is about timing. And about scheduled pastoral care visits. And also about embracing the unexpected.

21. "I know who I am"

A chaplain naturally serves as a catalyst for what religion means to hospital patients.

And the varied responses of patients to my presence are wondrous indeed.

For example, a 58-year-old black Baptist minister and ecclesiastical official, in an intensive care unit, invited me to sit down, and began to tell me what religion means to him. "God is love," he said. "God loves Muslims. Abraham was a Muslim. God loves the Muslims and the Jews and the Christians and everyone." He went on, "God loves black people and white people and Hispanic people and Chinese people."

The patient was just getting warmed up. "God does not hate. Those who use God to war against others are distorting God's love." I continued to listen. "God is a spirit, and a spirit cannot hate. Jesus said that we are to worship God 'in spirit and truth.' Hatred comes from peoples' own hearts, not from the heart of God; for God is love." It was like sitting and listening to a sermon—an inspiring one.

Then came the climax. The patient put his finger on the human heart, and its tendency to either love or hate. He said that an Admitting Department staff person told him that the hospital has Catholic and other chaplains, and asked whether he would want a chaplain to visit him. He replied, "Any of them can visit me. *I know who I am.*" My prayer, offered toward the end of the visit, gave thanks for who he is, and for who his god is, and for who others are.

It is in knowing who we are, "in spirit and truth," that prepares us to recognize and affirm others *as they are*.

This patient has numerous kindred religious spirits in the hospital. One is the Pentecostal sister of a 58-year-old black Baptist patient, whom I met in an intensive care unit waiting room. She started right off: "I didn't knowed my sister was Baptist. But that's not important. God loves us all. The main thing is how you treat others," she said. "That's gonna determine if you make it. Not anything else," she emphasized. "Love God and your neighbor as yourself. That's it! Whether you're good to others, because God loves everyone." "That's the Golden Rule," I replied. "That's right," she said. "And that's what it's about." Her final words: "If people don't treat others well, they ain't gonna make it."

To this sister, religion is about love, not language. It is about goodness, not grammar. About ethics, not education. About humanology, not theology. Perhaps she and the Baptist minister, and so many other black patients especially, reveal that the Golden rule is a bottom line of religion because of their history of being on the bottom in our society's white-controlled hierarchy of access to economic and political power.

A 65-year-old white woman patient had quite a different response to my presence and question, "Are you affiliated with a religion?" "No," she replied, and added apologetically, "I'm sorry." "Don't be sorry," I said.

A number of patients are apologetic about not belonging to or attending a church, as if religion is equated with church and attendance—of which, as chaplain, I'm a reminder. On occasion, in response to a certain patient's "I'm sorry"-like reply, I will jokingly say, "I'm not here to take church attendance," which usually gives both of us a laugh. Jesus said, "The Sabbath was made for people, not people for the Sabbath." (Mark 2: 27, International Standard Version) Translated: churches are made for people, not people for churches. Many patients are far more religious than they may realize, because religion is about the Golden Rule and not about the "gold" that rules those religious organizations committed to perpetuating their power and position and profit as guardians of the status quo. Nor does one need to give a religious interpretation to behavior for it to be legitimate and emulated.

Then there is the spontaneously honest 21-year-old white woman patient, whose religion was unknown, and who was surrounded by four or five family members. "I'm Rev. Alberts, hospital chaplain," I said upon entering her room. She burst out laughing. Then her family started laughing. And I laughed. When their laughter subsided, I said, "I used to do comedy on the side." All of them burst out laughing again. The young woman patient then said, "I'm not religious *at all*." "I respect that very much," I replied. For her, religion was a laughing matter, and I was its comedian. Somewhere along the way religion may have played "jokes" on her, or did not otherwise enable her individuated development and integrity as a woman.

Later, I said hello to the patient and her family as they entered the elevator on which I was riding. "I really did do comedy," I said to the patient, smiling, and added, "at a Chinese restaurant, in Harvard Square, Cambridge." She laughed, and said, "I thought you were joking." "I was joking," I said laughing, "and I did do comedy." As we walked out of the elevator together, the patient's mother turned to me and said, "Tell me one of your jokes." I did a mental check of my routine, and could not come up with a one-liner. "I can't think of one right now," I replied. She smiled, and then headed for the door and some sun and fresh air with her family.

A few minutes later I thought of a joke—that had more than one line. "I want to be the cleric of comedy. The pastor of the pun. The minister of mirth. The deacon of daffiness. The god of gags. The Jehovah of jokes. The lord of laughter." To which my son, Jeff, once replied, "And the bishop of the bomb." A prophetic response. My aspiring career as "the cleric of comedy" soon ended. Fortunately I kept my "day job" as a minister.

"Laughter is the best medicine." As are love and the Golden Rule and the spontaneous honesty embodied in the lives of patients and their loved ones.

22. "Could you say a prayer for me?"

The request did not come from a patient but from a nurse. I had just visited her patient, a 42-year-old white male who eventually was able to tell me his religion is Greek Orthodox. He was concerned about his laptop computer. "It's only a year old," he said. "I left it somewhere. There's a slight chance it's in the back of my truck," he added. He began to sit up, and lean forward, putting pressure on the strap that was keeping him from falling out of bed. He kept staring across the room, as if his computer might be over there. He also said something that indicated his unawareness of where he was, which led me to tell him, "You're at Boston Medical Center."

I asked what seemed like a natural question: "Do you have a co-worker who might check and see if you left the computer in your truck?" "No," he replied. I continued, "Do you have family whom you could ask to help you locate the computer?" "I have a mother and a father," he said, and then proceeded to give an unintelligible example of their apparently unhelpful behavior, which he summed up with, "That's the way they talk." His preoccupation and confusion led me to tell him that I would share his concern about his computer with his nurse.

His nurse was just outside his room, and evidently overheard our conversation. When I told her that the patient was preoccupied with the possibility of losing his computer, she smiled, and replied, "So that's the latest thing he's obsessed about. He has a lot of things like that on his mind. He's withdrawing from alcohol, and doesn't know where he's at." She then said, "I'm just waiting for the 60 milligrams of valium I gave him to hit him so *I* can relax." While she was speaking, I could see the patient busily moving about in his bed.

The nurse then said with a smile, "Could you say a prayer for me? I need it." I smiled in return and replied, "Sure. May you have a good day. And may all that is loving bless you very much." "Thank you, I need that," she said, smiling. She then said, "When his mother and father come in to see him, I will tell them about the computer."

Later, as I passed the nurse in the unit, she said with a smile, "Keep praying." "I will," I replied, smiling.

The nurse reveals our common human need for the very caring we caregivers provide for others.

23. 24/7

The pager went off at 2 a.m.; an un-welcomed awakening sound. A 53-year-old Catholic women had just died, and her male partner wanted to talk to a chaplain, and it did not matter whether the chaplain was a priest or a minister. [The patient had received the Anointing of the Sick a few days earlier.] "I'm sorry to call you at this hour," the nurse said apologetically. I replied, "That's okay. Human need is 24/7. I'm happy to talk with him." Before transferring the call to the deceased patient's room where her partner was, the nurse said, "I want to warn you that he is kind of slow." I sat down on a chair, rubbed my eyes, and waited for his "Hello."

The 51 year-old grieving man was soft-spoken and hesitant—and very human. He thanked me for my expression of sympathy, and then said, "Mildred and I have been together for 25 years, and now I'm all alone." "What is your biggest concern now?" I asked. He replied, "I'm afraid of, ah, I'm afraid of becoming isolated." "Do you have anyone you can talk to?" I asked. "Yes," he said, "I attend an anxiety group." I encouraged him to continue attending the group, which he planned to do. And he responded positively to my suggestion that he might want to consider talking with the female Catholic chaplain who provided pastoral care for his partner and him-- a woman who is very perceptive and caring.

There was also the offer of a prayer, over the telephone, which he readily accepted. It went something like, "God of love, you know John is very sad and fearful of becoming isolated. You love him and Mildred very much, and their love is sacred to you. She is ever and always with you; and you are always near and loving of him. And we thank you for the people with whom we can talk when we become fearful. Amen."

John expressed our common human condition of the pain of grief in losing a loved one and the ensuing fear of being alone. Pastoral care is about being there for people to talk to and with. Being a friend is about being there.

24. Honoring Diversity in Patient Care

Presented at the Nov. 1, 2008 annual meeting of the Massachusetts Memorial Hospital Nurses' Alumni Association. The Massachusetts Memorial Hospital became Boston University Medical Center, which, in turn, merged with Boston City Hospital to form Boston Medical Center.

I'm honored to join with you again to memorialize the nurses of your Association who have died during the last year.

I want to begin by reading Boston Medical Center president and CEO Elaine Ullian's January 2008 Diversity Statement. I believe the nurses we are memorializing today, and you also, embody the health care and human values contained in Mrs. Ullian's Statement:

Boston Medical Center is proud to be an integral part of the diverse community of Boston. It is this community, that is comprised of people from a wide variety of cultures and backgrounds, that the Medical Center draws upon as a resource for its employees as well as for patients.

As part of its stated mission and values, the Medical Center remains committed to creating and sustaining a work place and a hospital where employees, patients, and patients' families are respected and valued not in spite of, but because of, the differences in their backgrounds and cultures. We believe that there is strength in diversity, not only of race, gender, age, religion, and disability, but also of education, politics, family status, national origin, sexual orientation, and all of the other factors that make people individuals.

Honoring the diversity of our community will promote and ensure the mutual respect, collaboration, and productivity, which is necessary to provide the highest quality health care.

The nurses we memorialize today, and you as well, have honored the diversity of patients and their families from the first time they and you reached out to a patient in pain. You discovered right away that pain is no respecter of religious or political belief or wealth or title or race or gender or sexual orientation. Pain humanizes us.

The nurses we honor today, and you, learned early on that no mortal is exempt from mortality. That all of us laugh and cry. That all of us are human together. All of you have honored the diversity of patients with the knowledge that the hospital is the crossroads of our common humanity.

The nurses we honor today had much wisdom, as do you. If we could only see our assumed enemy cry and mourn. If we could only see those of another race or religion or nationality anxious and fearful. If we could only see them hope and struggle, laugh and love.

You nurses especially embody the diversity prized in Mrs. Ullian's statement. Three weeks ago I was paged by the family of a dying patient in intensive care. The family consisted of one biological daughter and one adopted daughter and two adopted sons, all adults. I was there for three hours, with that family—as was their intensive care nurse for most of that time. The family reminisced about their mother, as she slowly gave in to her mortality. A school teacher and librarian, who even had these daughters and sons as her students, and made sure they did their homework—and who favored the one adopted son they all lovingly recalled. With their mother as their teacher, it was kind of hard to feign sickness or play hooky. Who would write the excuse? Who would read it?

The intensive care nurse was there answering their questions regarding their mother's condition as life slowly ebbed from her. At one point, the one adopted daughter said to the nurse and me, "Thanks, you guys, for hanging in with us. It really helps." You could tell how closely they had bonded with the nurse by the way they said her name, "Carline." You could also tell by the way she responded. The nurse was of a different race than the daughters and sons and the patient. All of us human together in the face of death.

"Honoring the diversity of our community." All of us human together in the face of life. Like the two months old great-grandson of a Jehovah's Witness patient I've visited here often. Recently, that little great-grandson was outside the patient's room, being held by her granddaughter as the great-grandfather/patient's husband was standing nearby. I looked at the baby and then at the smiling great-grandfather and said, "Another flower is blooming." He enthusiastically replied, "Yes! Yes!"

"Honoring the diversity of our community." Around sixteen years ago a Jehovah's Witness patient inadvertently received a blood transfusion, which violated his religious beliefs and was a traumatic experience for him and his family—and for our medical team as well. This incident led the intensive care unit nurse manager, who was chair of the Nurses' Ethics Committee, to call a special meeting of the Committee, with Jehovah's Witness leaders in attendance. These leaders shared Jehovah's Witness beliefs related to health care. They also requested being able to visit Jehovah's Witness patients in the hospital. I attended that meeting. And it was the chair and the Nurses Ethics Committee who worked out the arrangement with me so that Jehovah's Witness elders could visit patients of their faith. And, with the patient's permission, we of the Pastoral Care Department have been informing Jehovah's Witness elders when members of their congregations are patients here ever since that Nurses' Ethics Committee meeting.

"Honoring the diversity of our community." Surely that diversity includes animals as well. Another intensive care nurse had to put her aged dog to sleep, which was a painful loss to her. In time, she got a puppy of the same mixed breed, which she affectionately calls her "little monster." In a short time, she discovered that her "little monster" had a kidney problem that would shorten his life to seven or eight years. When I expressed regret, she replied, "He's going to have the best seven or eight years of his life." Her patients also get that kind of care from her.

The nurses we memorialize today have "honor[ed] the diversity of our community"—and "provide[d], as Mrs. Ullian stated, "the highest quality health care" to patients and their families. We commend these nurses with deep gratitude to the god of life and love who walks on everyone's pathway.

The diversity of divinity. The divinity of diversity.

25. "What does she want on it?"

Presented at the November 3, 2007 annual meeting of the Massachusetts Memorial Hospital Nurses' Alumni Association.

God is love. God is love because God is big enough to transcend our theological, cultural, ethnic, national, racial and ideological differences and love all of us.

God is on all our pathways, not just one or some.

We call God by different names, and God calls each of us by our own name.

God is love. God creates, sustains and renews all of life. God's loving spirit is creative, affirming, renewing. God is the loving life-force of the universe.

God is love, and I see that love throughout the hospital.

I see God's love creating and sustaining the two plants on the altar of our Interfaith Chapel. Two plants that have been there for around 16 years; life flowing from their roots through their stems and petals, symbolizing the creative life-giving spirit of God at the center of the universe.

I see God as I cross the 2nd floor bridge from Collamore to the Atrium Building. On a cold cement ledge outside a window. In the raw early days of spring, exposed to the elements, a pigeon has built a nest from twigs and leaves and is sitting on two eggs. And, with the warmth and instinctual love of her body, brings to birth new life. And nourishes her young until they can fly. The warmth of love. I see God in such a loving birth in the face of that which is impersonal and even hostile to life.

I see God in the sound of Code Blue. Nurses and doctors and other staff running to a room in an effort to save a patient's life. Doesn't matter which patient. Or his or her religion, race, nationality, sexual orientation or social class. It is about the preciousness of every patient's life, and the commitment to revive and sustain his or her life. I see God in "Exceptional care. Without exception" [Boston Medical Center's motto].

I see God in an intensive care nurse's desire that a patient who has just died and has no family, not be alone. At that nurse's request, she and I stood by the patient's bedside, and I offered prayer—to the God of love who reveals that every human being is precious and to be cared for.

Finally, I hear God in the words of another intensive care nurse. A daughter came to visit her mother. The daughter is diabetic, was unable to eat anything before arriving at the hospital, felt somewhat ill, and asked me if there was a place on the unit where she could make toast for herself. I said I'd go ask her mother's nurse. When I did, the nurse replied, "I'll make it for her. What does she want on it?" I was moved by such exceptional caring.

God is love. And the hospital reveals the infiniteness of God's love. The hospital especially is such a human crossroads of our lives: it reveals our diversity and our connectedness, our individuality and our commonality, our uniqueness and our oneness.

"What does she want on it?" I believe these words especially reveal the loving spirit of the nurses whose lives we remember and honor and celebrate today.

"I'll make it for her. What does she want on it?"

26. "You're scaring me"

A major emotion hospitalized people and their families deal with is fear. Fear that the loved one may die or become disabled. And the chaplain, who, for many, represents the "last rites" for the living, may intensify this fear merely by his or her very presence. Thus upon entering a patient's room, I immediately introduce myself and clearly state that I'm making my rounds on the floor. The fact that I'm making rounds communicates to most patients that the visit is routine, rather than their thinking that they are being singled out for special attention, fearing, as one patient, supposedly joking, revealed in saying, "You're the chaplain? Am I that ill?" The aim is to put patients and their families at ease. But the following visit reveals the extent to which fear can distort what is being said and seen.

The 55-year-old intubated black patient's religion was unknown, and his wife was present in his intensive care unit room. Upon introducing myself and my routine visit on the unit, I told the patient's wife that his religion was unknown and asked if he were affiliated with a religion. She hesitated, and then said, "Yes," looking concerned. Usually the "Yes" is followed by the person identifying the affiliation, but not with her. I continued, "May I ask his religion?" She hesitated again, then replied, "Christian." "Catholic?" I asked. "No," she replied. Her apparent apprehension led me to explain, "I visit Christians who are not Catholic." Becoming more anxious, she said, "You're scaring me."

Now she was beginning to scare me. The role of a chaplain is to reassure patients and their families not frighten them.

Seeking to reassure the patient's wife, I repeated, "I'm Rev. Alberts, hospital chaplain, just making my rounds on the unit. And when a patient's religion is unknown, I seek to find that out. I would just want to give your husband a blessing." She replied, "Our pastor was here yesterday, and prayed with him." "That's wonderful," I replied "That's what I do as a chaplain, like your pastor." I then said, "May your husband enjoy rest and good progress in his treatment, and the Lord's blessing." "Thank you," she said, her face softening. "I also want to wish you a good day too," I added. "Thank you," she repeated, with a relaxed smile.

A few days later I visited the patient, who had been moved to another unit, and his wife was again present. He had progressed quite well, and was preparing to be discharged. Upon greeting them, I said to his wife, with a smile, "I remember you." "I remember you, too," she replied, smiling in return. "You and your husband were on 8 North when I was making my rounds, and I scared you," I said. She laughed, and said, "Yes," and added, with a smile that lighted up her face, "I'm not scared anymore." "Good," I replied. I then wished her husband much renewed health—to which she replied," I'll say 'Amen!' to that."

Fear is a powerful reminder of our shared humanity. It can lead us to distort reality or see it more clearly. It can lead us to become unnecessarily defensive or appropriately protective. It can lead us to become unduly suspicious of people, or deepen our understanding of them in knowing what it is like to be afraid.

Chaplaincy involves helping patients and their loved ones come to grips with fears that are gripping them—which begins with us chaplains coming to grips with our own fears.

"I will say 'Amen!' to that," too.

27. Chaplaincy Is About Helping Patients *Get* Better, Not *Be* Better

Mr. Jones is an 87-year-old white Protestant, World War II Navy veteran, who served as a radioman on a destroyer escort in the North Atlantic. He was delighted to hear that I, too, served on a destroyer escort as a signalman in World War II, and also in the North Atlantic. My visit with him was like a reunion between two former shipmates. The rapport established was almost immediate, and provided a cushion for navigating the emotionally laden mines floating inside him.

I evidently got too close to the first of three mines he directed my way. He and his wife and son, who were present, are members of a church that is looking for a new minister. "They may hire a woman," he began. "That won't go over well with some of the members." "Why is that?" I asked, anticipating a negative answer. "Women aren't meant to be ministers. It's in the Bible, you know," he said. Mr. Jones obviously was having difficulty cutting the "umbiblical" cord of patriarchy. I could have been more discerning.

"It may be in the Bible," I replied, "but people get used to it." I continued, "Years ago The United Methodist Church felt that way, and today there are even women bishops in Methodism." I then sympathized. "But I know what you mean: finding a minister that most people like is very important." "Yes," he replied. "It's been two years, and we're still without a minister." My being a fellow shipmate may have softened his conflicting feelings about women being ministers.

Mr. Jones excitedly talked about his Navy life, at times his thoughts too quick for his words, causing him to pause and stutter and repeat himself in an effort to catch up with his effusiveness. I enjoyed listening to him, and briefly shared my own World War II Navy experience.

Mr. Jones commented more than once about a sister destroyer

escort, sailing with his ship that was sunk by a German submarine a few days before the end of World War II. Many men on this ship were his friends. In fact, the captain of that ship wanted him to become chief radioman on the ship. "If I had done that," he said, "I wouldn't be here today."

It may have been Mr. Jones's anxiety over whether he would still be here tomorrow that led to his stream of talk, possibly driven by anticipation of the procedure on his heart he would undergo later in the afternoon. He evidently also enjoyed reminiscing with a [now] old Navy buddy about a very meaningful part of his life-- at a time when, as his son said to both of us, "There are fewer and fewer World War II veterans left."

I wanted Mr. Jones to know my age, as I thought it might provide some reassurance for him, facing a procedure and possibly thinking that his age may indicate he is at the end of his life. I noted that he was 87, and said, "You are only three years older than I am." "That's all?" he asked in disbelief.

Mr. Jones then floated another mine my way. "I don't like the president," he said. I heard him correctly, but needed a few seconds to deactivate his words. "Our president?" I asked. "Yes," he said. "Oh, you mean our president, President Obama." "Yes," he said. I was about to gently drop this mine over the side by ignoring it with a smile, when his son knowingly said, "Come on, dad. Let's not get into politics, or you'll be at it for an hour." A loving son who knows the ebb and tide of his loving father's ways.

There was a third mine to navigate. Mr. Jones was a policeman for 30 years. "I could only go so far up the ladder," he said, "because I was not a Catholic. I finally made it to lieutenant for a year before I retired." His sympathetic son commented, "That's the way it was in those days. But it's different now." I nodded, thinking to myself about a much earlier history when starving Irish Catholics came to America and were told not to apply for jobs, including on the police force—the tragic and all too common irony of oppressed groups overcoming their oppression and then using their power to oppress another group.

I offered to say a prayer during the visit. Mr. Jones responded positively, and then kept talking. Finally his wife interrupted him, saying, "Charles, the chaplain has offered to say a prayer. Let's stop and let him do it."

As I was about to leave, Mr. Jones kept bringing up new subjects. "I will come back again," I said. "Okay," he replied, then added, as I headed for the door, "If you see any Catholics, convert them." He then smiled. I stopped, thought for a second, re-entered his room and said, "I can't do that." I then added with a smile, "Nor would I want anyone to try to convert you." He and his wife and son chuckled affirmatively.

Chaplaincy is about where the patient is at, not the chaplain. It is about confidence-gaining and confidence-building, not conscience-keeping. It is about empathy, not ethics. About caring, not controlling. It is about the patient's opinion, not the chaplain's possibly differing belief. It is about acceptance and grace, not right belief and behavior. Chaplaincy is about helping a patient *get* better not *be* better.

28. The Empowerment of Being Understood

Belief that one is being understood by another is indispensable to confidence-building, problem-solving, and growth—and health. The helpless baby who is picked up and soothingly hugged by parents rather than left to cry. The fearful child who lies in order to get along with threatening adults. The anxious teenager struggling with embarrassing issues of personal identity. The worrying adult out on an economic limb with nowhere to turn. The concerned and angry patient and family for whom treatment has not gone as planned.

A 77-year-old black male Baptist patient, for example, underwent assumed routine surgery, had an unexpected stroke, and was dying. His shocked sisters and nephew expressed considerable anger at a family meeting: "He just came in for this surgery," one said. "He was all-right when he got here. Now look at him. He's dying! He may be just a patient to you, but he's *our brother and uncle.*"

Sympathetic staff persons tried to reassure the family that the medical treatment of the patient was thorough, that strokes after surgery, while uncommon, do occur, and that the patient may have had an unknown medical condition that contributed to the stroke. The intellectual, rational, and probably accurate explanations of what possibly happened did not console the family. What seemed to be helpful in shedding light on their feelings of shock and anger was my reflecting how they must feel in assuming their loved one was undergoing routine surgery, then suddenly seeing him dying from a stroke. The pastoral relationship I already had established with the sisters and nephew evidently contributed to whatever degree of being understood they felt at that family meeting. A primary challenge was to hear and understand and reflect their feelings—which may be more difficult if one's own feelings are unduly pressuring one to convince a family of one's best medical efforts.

The importance of understanding is also seen in a family meeting at which three daughters were discussing, with the attending doctor and other staff, their critically ill 82-year-old white mother's wishes regarding her terminal care. The doctor was very concerned to be guided by the patient's wishes. But the patient was having difficulty communicating her wishes. In an attempt to be helpful, another staff person talked about his mother's terminal care in a residential treatment center, and used his experience to suggest the daughters might consider a similar kind of terminal care for their mother. The suggestion led one of the daughters to react, "I find your suggestion offensive. This isn't about you and your mother." Unfortunately the staff person put himself in the daughters' place rather than discovering where they were.

Before ending the family meeting, the attending doctor, who valued and utilized the role of us chaplains, asked if I had any final words. My words were: "The daughters love their mother very much, and are very concerned that the treatment their mother receives is guided by her wishes."

On another occasion, I had the privilege of observing a doctor talking with a husband about the importance of being guided by the wishes of his 65-year-old wife, who only had a few months to live. The husband asked if it were more helpful to keep from his wife the amount of time she may have left, to make it easier for her—and for him. The doctor said, "It is better for her to know how long she has to live. She can then complete what is important for her in the time she has. If she doesn't know until near the end," the doctor continued, "what is important to her will be left undone, and her dying will be that much more difficult for her and for you. She may also feel that she has been deceived." The doctor's advice helped the husband to see more clearly what dying meant to his wife, and thus to deal more appropriately with his own feelings about her dying.

The empowerment of patients and their families is enhanced by their realization that they are being understood. Thus pastoral care is about understanding. Understanding where we chaplains are coming from in order for us to know where patients and their families are at.

Being understood is a universal human need. It enables growth and grieving, caring and community.

29. "Exceptional Care" in the Cafeteria and the Chapel

Two women broaden the meaning of Boston Medical Center's stated mission of providing "Exceptional Care. Without Exception." You won't find them in hospital beds or outpatient clinics, as they are not patients. The one, Mary, who is white and in her early eighties, may be seen, on any given day, in the cafeteria, where, for years, she has been greeting staff and gathering them under her wings. The other is Julia, a black woman in her sixties, who may be found every Sunday in the hospital's Interfaith Chapel, attending the weekly ecumenical service I lead. Both women have much to teach us about caring.

For Mary, who lives alone, it is not about lunch but about the people who eat lunch. It is about family. Her mother died at Boston Medical Center many years ago, which evidently led her to continue coming back to the place where she last saw her mother alive. Instead of the cemetery, it's a cafeteria which is filled with the living. People who have become her family.

A small, gregarious and outgoing woman, Mary sits at the same table every day, and makes the rounds of greeting numerous staff, most by name, she has come to know over the years, including my wife and me. She plays the role of hostess, straightening chairs under the tables, refilling the napkin containers, making sure enough utensils are available. I don't get napkins from the holders anymore. "Bill!," she calls out, "Over here! I got your napkins." Thanks, Mary." I respond. My wife and I usually eat lunch together. And if either of us in late, Mary will tell the one of us where the other is: "Eva, Bill is sitting over there."

Mary can be abrupt, and turn a person off with her frank demeanor. But underneath is a sensitive and caring woman, looking for and finding a family, at noon each day before she goes home to be alone.

Mary's need and Boston Medical Center's inclusive mission are perceptively captured in a birthday card a wise nurse gave to her, which Mary proudly showed to others and to me. The nurse wished Mary a happy birthday, wrote that she was a very special person, and ended her note with, "Thank you for taking care of us."

Julia is another woman who takes care of people in her own way. She has very little economic means, receives public assistance, and lives in public housing, which seemed to take her forever to secure. For years she came to the ecumenical service, living in the YWCA while looking for housing. Her patience and persistence in seeking her own place embody the very faith that the Interfaith Chapel seeks to inspire.

Julia has no family in the area. There is a friend, with whom she may share a Thanksgiving dinner and celebrate Christmas. Her biggest travels are a day trip to the Cape or to New Hampshire—to sit by the ocean or see the sights.

Like Mary, Julia also found a home at Boston Medical Center. A community to which she has given a lot while having so little. Years ago, she began putting an envelope containing money on the Interfaith Chapel's altar at Thanksgiving, then at Christmas, and again at Easter. In time, the amounts grew from $10 to $25 and now to $50. The money is used to buy palms for Palm Sunday, Easter lilies for the altar, poinsettia plants at Christmas, copies of The Koran for Muslim patients, Bibles for persons attending Catholic Masses, and for other pastoral care needs. With Julia sitting in the back pew, I delight in announcing, "The Easter lilies on the altar today are given by a dear friend of the Interfaith Chapel." Who would ever guess that Julia has provided a discretionary fund for the Pastoral Care Department at Boston Medical Center for some 15 years.

Once a security officer stopped Julia from attending a Sunday ecumenical service, having determined that she was an outsider and did not belong in the hospital. The issue of Julia's presence was quickly resolved.

Julia is there. Every Sunday. With so little. Giving so much.

Mary and Julia make a world of difference. Because nobody is an outsider in a world where there is the exceptional caring that says, "Thank you for taking care of us."

30. I'm sorry to go on like this, Chaplain. You probably came to talk about the church."

I was paged by a medical student to visit a 90-year-old black Pentecostal patient who had a lot on her mind. The medical student said that she had been crying and feeling afraid and had a history of depression, which led him to ask if she wanted to talk to a psychiatrist; but her preference was a chaplain. It became clear that she wanted to talk to someone who would listen, which a psychiatrist could do very well. But the patient evidently felt more comfortable with a chaplain.

Being diabetic, the patient expressed considerable concern about her foot. About her fear of losing her toes and possibly her foot. About where she would be living: back at her longtime senior citizens' building apartment or in a nursing home. About, "I don't know where I'll be," adding, "They ask me not to say that."

The patient then went into detail about a nurse who was mistreating her, she said. She acted out the nurse's perceived disparaging manner: "Do you want the bed pan?" and repeated the question impatiently after the patient already had said, "I just used it." "Do you want me to get anything from the kitchen?" the nurse repeated, and in a demanding tone, "Tell me now. Tell me now." The patient responded that she already had eaten.

The nurse's perceived grudging and insistent manner led the patient to criticize her: "A young woman talking that way to an older person." The patient told her very protective grandson, who called the unit and complained to the nurse. The nurse later came into the patient's room and denied talking disparagingly to her. The believed inappropriate treatment evidently stopped, as the patient saw no need to accept my suggestion that she could share her complaint with the hospital's patient advocate.

The patient said, "If you can't deal with the public, you shouldn't be working with the public." She spoke from personal experience. "I

83

was a health care aide during and after the end of World War II. I worked with all kinds of people," she continued, "Indians, Asians, and others, the women that veterans met and married overseas and brought back." She also worked as a health care aide for a social service agency in the Boston area.

The patient enjoyed talking. At times, she would smile, lean forward, and look me in the eyes for effect. One of the indicators of her clarity was her ability to name all of her eight siblings in succession.

There is more. The patient continued, "I worked in homes all over Greater Boston." She then said, with a smile of integrity crossing her face, "I never touched anything that belonged to people in whose home I worked. People would mislay things, and I'd find them. Some people," she went on, "would lay out money just to see if I would take it, and I never did."

Deep into my visit with the patient, she suddenly interrupted herself, leaned forward, looked directly into my eyes, touched my arm, and said, "I've been going on and on here. You probably came to talk about the church." "No," I replied. "I'm here for you to talk about whatever is important to you."

31. "I was a hopeless drug addict. Now I'm a dopeless hope addict."

He is a 31-year-old white Italian Christian with Crohn's Disease, who reveals the power of belief to transform behavior—as well as the exclusiveness of a belief driven by the need for certainty. When I entered his room and identified myself, he greeted me warmly, invited me to sit down, and began to tell his story.

"I could never hold a job," he said. "I did one thing after another." He became addicted to alcohol and drugs. Now he is an outreach minister, seeking to rescue young people with similar addictions. He said with a smile, "I like to say, I was a hopeless drug addict. Now I'm a dopeless hope addict." His words grabbed my attention.

"What turned you around?" I asked, anticipating his answer. "Jesus," he said. "He is my savior. I now have eternity in my heart, and have no fear of death. I have eternity in my heart," he repeated.

I asked what led him to Jesus. He replied, "Friends, whom God used to influence me." He attended youth evangelistic services with them. "It took some doing," he said. His preparation for outreach ministry included graduating from a Christian college.

The patient hoped that his illness would deepen his understanding and his faith. He found inspiration for this hope in Jesus telling his disciples to endure when they suffered persecution, for, "By your endurance you will gain your souls." (Luke 21: 12-19) I communicated an understanding of how suffering can deepen insight and faith, which he appreciated.

Toward the end of the visit, I held his hand and offered a prayer, which affirmed the preciousness of his life to his god, the importance of his ministry in seeking to help others addicted to alcohol and drugs, and the preciousness of their lives as well. The prayer also held up his hope that out of his illness would come greater understanding and faith. All "in Jesus' name." As I ended the visit, he said, "I will be here for a few days," and invited me back.

During the second visit, I entered into a rare discussion of my beliefs with the patient. My answers to his growing interest in me and my chaplaincy led him to say, "Maybe members of my ministry could come and lead a Sunday service in your chapel. We could probably help people who are addicted to alcohol and drugs here." I replied that such a service would not be appropriate in the hospital because of the various religious pathways of patients—"Jews, Muslims, Hindus, Buddhists, and Christians of various beliefs, and people of no religious beliefs." "Just thought I'd ask," he said. "No harm in asking." "Of course not," I replied.

The patient then revealed the inability of belief driven by the need for certainty to affirmingly differentiate between people. He stated, "Jesus said that he is the only way. No one else. There's only one way to have eternity in your heart." He was referring to Jesus recorded as saying in John 14: 6, "I am the way, and the truth, and the life. No one comes to the Father except through me." He then asked, "Do you believe that people can find eternity in their heart without him?" I replied, "Yes. I believe people are born with eternity in their heart. All are eternally precious. All are sacred."

I then reminded the patient that Jesus said, "Love your neighbor as yourself. He replied, "I believe that." I responded, "Up to a point. But then you want people to believe like yourself, rather than be who they are." He made no response.

I rarely become involved in a theological discussion with a patient or family members. My role as a chaplain is to be supportive and to utilize a patient's faith to help him or her cope with illness or injury. In the patient's case I made an exception, partly because of the rapport we had established—seen in his warm greetings of "chaplain" and "pastor," in his invitations for me to sit down, in his open sharing of himself, and in his receptivity to me and my prayers. It was also important to affirm to him the hospital as a *crossroad* of humanity and not an *inroad* for a cross.

The patient's inner conflict and related need to consume alcohol and drugs, rather than being resolved through belief, may have been transferred to a need to consume people with his belief. My continued visits and prayers, in which I focused on the progress of his recovery and the importance of his ministry, may have touched his need to believe that his own heart *is* eternally precious.

The power of belief to transform "a hopeless drug addict into a dopeless hope addict" is marvelous indeed. As is the liberating power of belief in the diversity of divinity and the divinity of diversity —

symbolized by a lotus flower adorning the center of the altar cloth covering the altar in Boston Medical Center's interfaith chapel.

But the bottom line of chaplaincy is not about belief but about caring for patients and their loved ones.

32. "Will it cost us more to have you come back a second time?"

I was paged by the nurse of a dying 79-year-old Hispanic Pentecostal woman, whose large, mostly bilingual, family had gathered in a visitor's room. When I arrived, around 20 family members filled the room, and the elder son was speaking to them in Spanish, as a teenage girl (possibly a grand-daughter) was kneeling and grieving near him. I had established contact with a grandson before entering the visitor's room, and he offered to assist and interpret for me. The elder son, recognizing my presence, asked me to wait until he finished. After ending the discussion of a family concern, he invited me to speak.

I introduced myself, said my intent was not to intrude, but to respond in any way they thought might be helpful. I added, "I can stay here and be with you and listen, if you wish. Or I can leave, and return later if you want me to come back. All you have to do is tell the nurse to page me again. It's what you want that's important to me." The family spokes-person son answered, "Will it cost us more to have you come back a second time?" "No," I replied. "I'm the hospital chaplain, and this is my work." The son replied, "We're busy now, but we would like you to come back later."

Around an hour-and-a-half later, I was paged to return at the family's request. The patient had just died, and her loved ones had surrounded her bedside, with her elder son stroking her forehead. When I entered the room, he said, "Would you like to say something?" I invited everyone to hold hands, and then offered a prayer that gave thanks to their god for the preciousness of the patient's life to them, and their lives to her, and her life to their god. This big, loving, and grieving family then continued to find comfort in each other's arms. Shortly the elder son came over to me, put his arm around my waist, as I then put my arm around him, and thanked me for my presence and prayer. He then said, "My mother kept us all together, and now everyone is worried that we will fall apart. But we will carry on."

After all the family members and friends said their good-byes to the patient and left the room, the elder son returned alone to say a final good-bye to his mother. He then returned from her room with tears in his eyes. As he walked by, he looked at me, and reached for and held my hand in a brief tight grip. Words cannot begin to describe the meaning of this mother's life to her son and her other loved ones. It is the tears that reveal something of the history and depth and power and pain of human love.

"Will it cost us more to have you come back a second time?" How many families, in the midst of overwhelming grief, are forced to struggle with the terrible financial cost of health care and dying in our inequitable society? A society whose government has over 1000 military bases around the globe, creating enemies rather than protecting America's security, and no universal health care that would really protect its citizens.

33. "I'm so thankful you are here"

A 52-year-old black United Methodist patient reveals the importance of taking the time to listen to people. He invited me to sit down, and then began to tell his story, which was punctuated by strong emotional feelings.

The patient had undergone 17 hours of open-heart surgery. He had ignored symptomatic gurgling sounds in his body, and continued to work for three days before finally coming to the hospital. He described a quick trip by ambulance to the operating room, and said, "I almost didn't make it," his voice choking up and his eyes becoming tearful.

The patient is an outreach technician working with homeless persons, which involves contacting them and enabling them to connect with needed services. "That is important work," I responded. "I think so," he said, his eyes watering.

The patient previously worked four years with mentally disadvantaged young people. Having a BA in child development and an MA in local and state government administration, he said, "I like to work for humanity. I'm committed to people. You shouldn't judge them." Experience with disadvantaged persons evidently contributed to his understanding and compassion, just as his seemingly compassionate make-up probably motivated his "commitment to people." His motivation is apparently seen in him saying that he had a job with the state, but decided that he liked hands-on work with people rather than being "a bureaucrat."

The patient said that his illness had dramatically changed his outlook. He intends to be more patient with himself and less bothered by circumstances beyond his control. His "almost" not "mak[ing] it," has led him to be even more convinced that "God is looking out for me."

When I said, "Would you like me to offer a prayer?" the patient said, "Of course, Reverend," his voice becoming husky as he reached his hand out for me to hold. The prayer affirmed him, and his doctors and nurses, and his own "commitment to people" and his good work with them, and all that sustains and renews him—"in Jesus' name and in the name of all that is loving."

I thanked the patient for sharing his story with me. He replied, "I'm so thankful that you are here, pastor," his voice breaking up a little. "Thank you," I responded.

A few days later, I visited the patient again. He stated that he was progressing well. I recalled the earlier visit saying, "You were expressing strong emotional feelings the last time." "Yes," he replied with a smile. After his discharge, a cousin who lives nearby "will be looking in on me," he said. And he may be able to return, part-time, to his work with homeless people, "my boss, who visited me, said," he stated.

The patient said, with a smile, "I told my sister about you." Oh, you have a sister too," I replied. "A sister in the church," he explained. "I told her that you were a godsend." "That's nice," I replied. He added, "Keep up the good work. It is very much needed."

The patient had evidently taken his life for granted, and is now deeply thankful to his god—and his doctors—for the new life he is being granted.

The patient exemplifies how listening can help a person verbalize strong feelings that need air and compassionate understanding. Such listening may help any person to endure and learn from struggles—and even gain a new lease on life.

The patient's story is also about faith that can help to sustain one's spirit and strengthen one's will to renew one's life—with the continuing blessings of a "cousin" and a "boss" and a "sister."

Chaplaincy is often not about providing answers but about asking questions and listening.

34. On Being Imperfect

Show me a perfect person and I will show you an imperfect human being. I take comfort in these words for good reason.

Recently I visited a 66-year-old white patient in an intensive care unit whose first name clearly sounded female. "Good morning, Mrs. Smith," I said upon entering the patient's room. The patient's son, who was sitting near the entrance said, "That's my father." "Oh, I'm sorry," I replied, feeling embarrassed. Upon looking more closely at the patient, I saw whiskers and other masculine bodily features. I immediately called him "Mr. Smith," and continued the visit, with a self-imposed cloud of embarrassment hanging over my head.

Afterwards, the patient's nurse helped me to remove the cloud. When I shared my mistake with her, she said, "It happens. In the hospital people can look differently." She also sympathized with my being misled by the feminine spelling of the patient's first name. The nurse's consoling words reminded me that we get to where we are going in a passenger ship and not in a canoe. The help of others along the way is precious indeed.

That same day I struggled to understand what a 34-year-old black male patient, in another intensive care unit, was trying to tell me. The patient, whose religion was unknown, was awake, but he was trached. I introduced myself and stated, as usual, that I was making my rounds on the floor and that my visit was routine. He nodded. I continued, "Your religion is not listed. Are you affiliated with a religion?" He nodded, and then tried to speak, but his words were indistinguishable—though I thought I heard a word starting with the letter "p". I asked, "Are you Protestant?" He shook his head, and repeated what he had tried to say. "Are you Pentecostal?" I continued. He shook his head, and again tried to pronounce the three words. "Are you Catholic?" He repeated himself. "I don't want to tax you," I said, hesitating. Then I asked, "Are you Baptist?" He shook his head. "Rastafarian?" He stared at me. As I was about to give up, he repeated his three words again. I finally thought I heard the word

92

"pray," and said, "Are you asking me to pray for you?" He nodded a vigorous "yes." Which led me to smile. I touched his arm with my hand and prayed for him. Which led him to smile. *I'm trying to find out his religion, and he's trying to tell me to pray for him.*

But waiting at another intensive care unit was a good laugh. It involved a 50-some-year-old white woman patient whose religion was not listed. "Are you affiliated with a religion?" I asked her. She hesitated, then replied, "So-so." She then laughed, and said, "That's the best I can do." "I don't have a category for 'so-so,'" I said. At which we both laughed heartily.

Laughter still provides some of the best medicine—and spirituality. It also helps us imperfect people feel like human beings.

35. Of Tattoos and Love

"Happy Mother's Day, Daniel," I said upon greeting a long-time weekend black hospital employee. "Hi, Reverend," Daniel responded, with a surprised "I'm-not-a-mother" smile. That Mother's Day greeting to him led to a remarkable conversation and discovery.

Having known Daniel for years, I've regularly inquired about and encouraged his college and graduate school studies and his ensuing career. Our relationship had grown to the point of him being able to share with me a troubling personal matter—a concern that I recalled upon wishing him a happy Mother's Day.

"Daniel," I said, "I remember you telling me a year or so ago that you wanted to get a tattoo. But your mother was opposed to it. Didn't she say that, like the Bible says, 'Your body is a temple of the Holy Spirit,' and that a tattoo would defile it?"

"Something like that," he replied.

I recalled him asking my opinion at the time, and my telling him that getting a tattoo is a personal decision, that it is difficult to get rid of if a passing fad, and that his mother was sharing what her religion taught her to believe. While tattooing reportedly has been practiced throughout the world for some 12,000 years BC, it was banned by Pope Hadrian in 787 AD. (See, "A Brief History of Tattoos," *www.powerverbs.com/tattooyou/history.htm*) And 19th century western missionaries condemned tattooing as unholy, forcing its decline in Polynesian societies. (See, "History of Tattoo," *www.pbs.org/skinstories/history/index.html*) The real sin, I believe, is "tattooing" one's own beliefs on another's person's mind, which is the temple of another's individuality, elaborative development and diversification.

The above recollection led me to ask, "Daniel, did you ever get a tattoo?"

"Yes," he replied. "Do you want to see it?"

"Sure," I said. With that, he pulled up the sleeve on his right arm, and there on his upper arm was a stately tattoo of the universally recognized Prayerful Hands. Struck by the symbolism, I asked why he chose the Prayerful Hands. He said, "In memory of my 11-year-old brother who died a year ago. "How did he die?" I asked. Daniel replied, "In an accident." I expressed sympathy.

"Has your mother seen your tattoo?" I asked. "No," Daniel replied. "When she comes to my place, I keep my shirt on and my sleeves rolled down. But I will be sharing it with her."

I said, "Maybe she won't be as upset when she learns what it symbolizes." He answered, "She'll have a fit."

May Daniel's mother come to realize that when she puts her arms around him, she is also hugging the eternal preciousness of her other son who is resurrected in Daniel's heart—and in her heart.

36. On Getting Close to People

I was paged to go to the room of a dying 40-year-old white male patient, and provide pastoral care for his white male friend of the same age. The friend was standing on the other side of the patient's bed. Rather than carry on a conversation across the bed, I went around to the friend's side, introduced myself and shook his hand-- and smelled the alcohol on his breath.

The patient was unresponsive. His treatment was extensive and his dying medically determined. And he was about to be transferred to another facility.

The two had known each other for three years, and had been in an alcohol recovery program together. And the patient "would give you the shirt off his back," the friend said. Now it was his turn to reciprocate: he was looking for pastoral support, as he believed the doctors were giving up on the patient.

The friend then demonstrated his belief: he went over to the patient, touched his forehead, and the patient's eyes fluttered. The friend repeated his action. "See," he said, "the doctor's are not picking up on this. I'm an EMT, and I've had some experience with this."

A short time later, a male staff person came into the room, and stood at the other side of the bed. When the staff person introduced himself, the friend made a forward movement to shake his hand. The staff person responded by putting his hands under his arms and taking a step backwards, which discouraged the friend's movement.

At the friend's request, a female resident, who had provided medical care for the patient, entered the room to respond to his concerns. She went around to his side of the bed, introduced herself and took the initiative to shake his hand. She listened to him and observed his demonstration of touching the patient's forehead. She then explained that the patient's response was an automatic nerve reflex and not indicative of a hopeful sign of life. She said that tests had been performed on him indicating no promising sign of life.

The friend still wanted to talk to the patient's attending doctor.

96

The resident arranged for the friend to talk with the doctor later by telephone.

After the resident and other staff person left the room, the friend talked more about his closeness with and love for the dying patient. Who, he repeated "would give you the shirt off his back."

Continuing to stand next to him, I said, "It must be very painful for you to see your friend like this." He responded that it was. Then he suddenly broke down and threw his arms around me and sobbed. I hugged and comforted him until he stopped crying.

The friend then said that he hoped he was not "rude" to the resident, and would apologize if he were "too pushy." I said he was not rude. Actually, beyond the smell of alcohol was a man who was rational, articulate and responsive—and mourning the dying of his friend. And no doubt mourning his sudden loneliness-- and possibly also his own dying mirrored by his friend. I told him that he was being a good friend in caring and advocating for his friend. And that his friend would want him to take care of himself.

Pastoral care involves getting close to people. And getting close to people involves getting close to people.

37. The "Snot-Nosed Kid" Who Was Loved

He was a black teenager. Shot in the head, at night on a Dorchester street, and rushed to Boston Medical Center. The hospital chaplain on call, I was paged at the request of his family, whose members were in shock.

The youth's father had difficulty containing himself, pacing back and forth in the hallway, now and then leaning against a wall with his head in his arms, and staring blankly when comfort was offered. When he finally sat down on a couch in the visitor's room, his mother-in-law stood behind him and caringly rubbed his shoulders to calm him.

The teenager's mother was fearful of entering her son's hospital room, but finally pushed herself to do so. Seeing her son prone and unconscious on the bed, she screamed. The pain of her own wounded love for him piercing the air. Overcome with fear, she fell to the floor, and was picked up and helped onto a chair by family members and hospital staff. Later, she was sitting in the visitor's room; and as I returned from her son's bedside, she continued to stare at me. Finally she fearfully asked, "Do you have something to tell us?" "No," I replied. "I'm just returning to be with you," sensing the dread behind her question.

The teenage youth's younger sibling sat just outside his room, keeping vigil and sobbing—stunned by the sudden violence that was ending the beloved brother's life. Their short, precious history together as siblings suddenly and senselessly ending in that hospital room. Staff took turns comforting the sibling.

The teenager's aunt stood next to his bed, gently siphoning the blood repeatedly oozing from his nose and the side of his mouth. At one point, as she siphoned blood coming out of his nose, she looked at him and lovingly said, "You always were a snot-nosed kid." She then gave a sad chuckle, as did the attending nurse on the other side of the bed.

In spite of the medical staff's exhaustive efforts, the teenager died early that spring morning, not long ago. His tragic death offers a warning and an opportunity, as summer arrives with its heated potential for street violence.

This young person—and his loved ones—put a human face on state legislatures' budgets for youth violence prevention programs and for safety net hospitals like Boston Medical Center. It should not be about cutting the budget and saving money during an economic crisis, but about serving vulnerable people in crisis and saving lives. It is about restoring funding for hospitals that provide comprehensive health care especially for those who have the least. It is also about fully funding statewide youth programs for those who are often last, so that they do not get lost. It is about a "snot-nosed kid" who was dearly loved, and who should not have had to die.

38. "This has been a pleasant surprise... Your Excellency"

As I entered the patient's room, the bathroom door, just inside the entranceway, was wide open, and a man was sitting on the toilet. I said, apologetically, "Oh, I'm sorry." His nonchalant response led me to pause long enough to introduce myself as the hospital chaplain and to ask, "Are you Jason Hopewell?" "Yes," he replied, and added, "I want to talk to you." "I will come back," I responded.

A white man in his thirties, the patient greeted me with, "Your Excellency," then sat on his bed with his legs crossed, and I took a chair. I've been called a lot of things in my time but never "Your Excellency." My initial aim was to obtain his religious preference, which was unknown. Saying he was Episcopalian, he immediately stated what he wanted to talk about: "I don't like certain of my feelings. And I want to get close to God." (His sudden, and possibly fleeting illness—he was discharged the next day—may have helped to motivate his desire for closeness with his god.)

"What feelings don't you like?" I asked. He replied, "I've been jealous of this man who is handsome. He became ill, and I found myself feeling good about his condition. I then got to know him better, and he seemed like a good person. I don't like myself for finding pleasure in his illness."

I said that his jealousy indicated he had feelings of insecurity about himself. That feeling good about himself would enable him to be more accepting of and compassionate toward other persons. I asked if that made sense to him. He said that it clearly did.

One's god can be a divisive weapon in the mind of an insecure and jealous person. Or a transcending inspiration in the heart of a self-aware and loving person. Thus I focused on the *relationship* between him not liking his feelings of jealousy and his desire to get close to his god: "I believe getting close to God involves getting close to yourself, i.e. understanding yourself. Your perception of God, like your feelings about other persons, can be colored by your own insecurities and any unresolved issues. Self-understanding, awareness and acceptance of your own humanness and working on personal issues—that's what I mean by getting close to yourself, which, I believe is a gateway to closeness with God." This statement gave him pause, and led him to reply, "You are getting close to home here." "Have you ever talked to a mental health professional before?" I asked. "Yes," he answered. "You may want to consider it again."

"What kind of work do you do?" I asked. The patient is a television news reporter, worked for a major network affiliate and has a job interview in a few days with a different affiliate. His training included working as a volunteer staff person for the lieutenant governor of a large eastern state. He enthusiastically described his work as a news reporter: "You're at the scene and center of events that are on the top of the news and in everyone's minds." He then explained how composing reports from the scene of a story is far more grammatically challenging than the reports written for an anchor person at the television station. He pointed out the importance for viewer interest of reporting from the actual scene of a story. He expressed interest in the value I placed in having personally utilized television media to cover newsworthy church involvements.

Because of the enthusiasm he displayed in describing his work as a television reporter, I asked, "What makes you happy?" He replied, "Feeling loved and safe." "Do you feel loved?" I asked. "Yes," he replied with no hesitation. He is apparently close to his sister and brother-in-law whom he was visiting in the Boston area when he became ill, and to his parents who continue to support him financially. I stated the enthusiasm with which he described his work as a television news reporter, and asked if obtaining such a position again might help him to feel safe. "Yes," he replied.

When I introduced the end of my visit, he said, "Say something to me in ten seconds or less." I answered, "May your self-understanding lead you closer to your own humanness. May you enjoy much love and safety. And best wishes in that television interview next week." He replied, "Thank you, Your Excellency. This has been a pleasant surprise."

39. "Take off your hats"

Immediately upon arriving at the hospital at 8 am, I was paged: a 79-year-old black woman, who was Baptist, had just died and her family was requesting the chaplain. I had participated in a family meeting the day before, at which the attending doctor told the many members gathered that their mother was no longer responding to dialysis treatment, that her diabetes was affecting her whole body, and that she probably had two weeks to live at the most. Her oldest son, a tall, burly man in his late 50s, believed she would die that evening, and stayed with her all night. They watched television together, with him holding her hand; and she was aware enough to be present with him. She died at 8 am, with him by her side.

As I entered the room, he immediately came to me and, with his big arms, enveloped me in a hug, and with tears in his eyes said, "I knew she was going to die last night, Reverend. We were together watching television. And this morning she was gone." "It is so good that you were with her," I responded. "I'm sure it meant much to her, as well as to you."

The oldest son continued the painful and difficult task of calling his many family members. Upon repeatedly dialing numbers and getting voice mail messages, he complained, "Why do they have a damn cell phone if they aren't going to turn it on?" His grief and frustration in seeking to reach his family told me that I should be with him, rather than attend to other matters and come back when everyone arrived later. He finally got a niece on the line and impatiently said, "Listen! Don't talk! Your grandma died this morning at 8 o'clock. Get your mom on the phone." To another relative, he said, "Mom just died. Get your butt over here!" He then stopped dialing, and began sobbing. I went over and put my hand on his shoulder and said, "This is very painful for you." He nodded, wiping away tears.

It took four hours for the family to gather at the patient's bedside. During this time, I responded to the oldest son's request by calling two Massachusetts correctional institutions in an attempt to inform two brothers of their mother's death. When the one incarcerated brother was informed that his mother had just died, he became aggressive, wanting to hit anybody, and had to be separated from the rest of the prison population. The other brother had become a Muslim and changed his name, which led me to obtain his correct commitment number by calling his wife, who was in Florida. During our conversation, I gave her the telephone number of her mother-in-law's room, which allowed her to talk with family members directly.

Some 15 to 20 family members gathered around their dead loved one's bedside, with her oldest son, standing closest to her, stroking her brow and offering a down-to-earth eulogy: "You are the best mother in the world. You were always there for us. Whether we were right or wrong, you protected us. *Always!*" He then said to those surrounding her bedside, "We have to do something about this diabetes. We have to protect ourselves. We pledge, Mama, that we're going to do something about it." "Yes," many responded.

Ironically, a February 5, 2006 *New York Times* editorial, called "Declare War on Diabetes," states, "Most of those who have diabetes have Type 2, in which obesity and poverty are key contributors, especially among blacks and Hispanics, who are disproportionately stricken... Diabetes is a disease defined by economic disparity."

There is also a relationship between the far higher percentage of black men incarcerated in prisons and America's historic white-controlled hierarchy of access to economic and political and legal power. The National Urban League's 288-page report, entitled, "State of Black America 2009: Message to the President," found, "Even as an African American man holds the highest office [in] the country, African Americans remain twice as likely as whites to be unemployed, three times more likely to live in poverty and more than six times as likely to be incarcerated." This mother had to "protect" her many children from an unequal environmental and educational and economic and political white-controlled playing field.

As the many family members gathered around their loved one's bedside, the oldest son asked me to offer a prayer, before which he ordered everyone to, "Take off your hats." It was about deep respect for the mother and grandmother and great-grandmother who "protected" her family and lived her life for them. It was a prayer that gave thanks for the preciousness of her life to them and to their god whose love never ends.

A short time later, the patient's great-grandson, a husky older teenager, marched into the room, looked at his dead great-grandmother, and immediately left in shock. The oldest son said, "Oh, oh. I thought so." He then proceeded to follow his grandson out of the room, with most of the other family members trailing behind him. They surrounded the great-grandson in the hospital unit's hallway, where he was overcome with grief. A perceptive nurse told us to take him to a private room in the unit, where family members sat him on a chair, and five or six of us at a time hugged and comforted him. He was sobbing and moaning loudly and his leg was shaking uncontrollably. Finally his physical tremors of grief subsided—*only* because many of his family members were there to hug and comfort him. The needed comfort of so many who surrounded him is a commentary on any hospital policy that limits family (and friends) visitors to two persons at a time. Such a policy may serve to protect other patients from potentially disruptive behavior of a crowd of people. But it may undercut the supportive roles family members and friends provide for each other at such a critical moment of great loss.

Fortunately, hospital policy accommodated this large, loving, grief-stricken black family. The oldest son talked comfortingly to his grandson, then helped him to his feet, and, with everyone following, gently led him back to his great-grandmother's room. They stood together by her bedside, with the great-grandson silently staring at her body. Then, without any word from his grandfather, he took off his hat, bent down and kissed his great-grandmother on the cheek, and quietly left the room.

40. "I miss her so bad."

John West is an 83-year-old white Episcopal patient, with congestive heart failure, whose wife of almost 60 years died six months ago. His doctor asked me to visit him, saying that his grief was very painful, leading him to express suicidal thoughts.

Upon introducing myself to Mr. West, and his son who was in the room, the son excused himself "so that dad can talk to you alone." (The son expressed appreciation later for his father being able to share his grief with me as a chaplain.)

"Mr. West," I began, "your doctor asked me to come by. She said your wife died recently and that you were together a long time." "Yes," he replied, "I still miss her very much." "The doctor said that you and your wife were together since you were very young," I continued. "We were together since we were 14 and 13 years old," he replied. I responded, "It's wonderful to be with someone from such an early age, but I'm sure your loss is very painful." "Yes," he replied. "I miss her so bad."

My questions sought to help Mr. West talk about his wife, if he wanted to share his grief with me. Evidently he did. And his sharing helped me to understand whether he might want to pre-maturely end his life in an attempt to be with her.

"What is your wife's name?" I asked. "Dorothy," he said. "Together since you were 14 and 13," I continued, "Where did you and Dorothy meet?" "In church, in a youth group," he replied. "And we were together ever since. I went to the high school in my town, and she went to the one in the next town over; but we were always together."

Seeking to learn more about his wife, I asked, "What was it about her?" "She was just great. We got along so well. Her ashes are at my son's house."

Mr. West suffered physical discomfort from his backside, occasionally moaning and moving his body. And at times his breathing was labored, and interrupted his speaking. At one point, when he looked tired and closed his eyes, I said that I did not want to tire him. He immediately replied that he was all right and wanted me to stay.

John and Dorothy were married while he was in the service, toward the end of World War II. He was a Marine drill sergeant. During the Korean War, he re-enlisted for 10 years; they were able to live together as he remained stateside. As a civilian, he did masonry work, helping to build shopping malls, and later became a deputy sheriff in a small town for 12 years. Along with his son, Mr. West has three granddaughters, two of whom are married and the third is about to receive her Master's degree. Our rapport was helped by my having been in the Navy during World War II, and by our having lived in the same area of the city for a period of time and knowing similar persons.

At the end of this first visit, Mr. West gladly accepted my offer of a prayer. In the prayer, I gave thanks for "the preciousness of the love John and Dorothy shared for so long, and still share," a love that will never end and is blessed by their eternally loving god, "who surrounds her even as she is also resurrected in John's heart." The prayer also revered the love that this patient shares with his son and three granddaughters, and gave thanks for all that nourished and sustained him.

In a subsequent visit, I wanted to pursue a statement Mr. West made that slid by me. He had said, "I don't know why I'm still here." I should have asked what he meant by that, thinking he might have been revealing a wish to die. Thus I recalled Mr. West's statement and asked its meaning. He replied, "I was wondering why I haven't left this place yet and gone to a rehab facility. I'm ready for the next adventure." "Which is?" I asked. "Getting out of here and getting to the next place." I said, "And after that, home?"

He answered, "Who the hell knows?" I said, "I'm sure you will be very happy when it is time to be reunited with your wife." He replied, "For sure. That is the best!" I responded, "Until then, you have your son and three granddaughters who love you and want you to be around as long as possible. You know that." "Yes," he said.

My closing prayer called on his god to bless his "new adventure," and gave thanks "for the love John and Dorothy will always share." He ended the visit by saying, "Thank you, sir. You have been a big help to me."

Mr. West's reality is his powerful wish to be re-united with is wife, Dorothy. To articulate that reality is to connect with and help him to express and relieve his grief. Pastoral care is about giving grief the hearing it needs rather than it remaining bottled up and beside itself.

41. "Are You Affiliated With a Religion?" "No, I'm Free."

Hospital chaplaincy is about making a patient's day. Tuning in. Listening. Affirming. It is about experiencing a patient's reality, not interpreting it. About where the patient is, and not where one thinks he or she should be. It is about a patient getting better, not becoming a better Christian or person. About perceiving the patient as an end in herself or himself, and not a means for promoting religion or church. *It is about the patient, not "God."* Still, while it is about the patients, often they make my day as a hospital chaplain, and I hope what they gave to me helped to make their day.

One is a 30-year-old black man in an intensive care unit whose religion was unknown. Upon entering his room, I said, "Good morning. I'm Rev. Alberts, hospital chaplain, making my rounds on the floor." He cheerfully replied, "Good morning, sir." I continued, "Your religion was not listed. Are you affiliated with a religion?" I've asked that question daily of patients for over 18 years, and have never received a response like his: "Am I affiliated with a religion? No," he replied. "I'm free." He then gave a full-bodied laugh. I responded with laughter, and said, "I appreciate that very much." Following which, a young woman, sitting by his window, pulled back the curtain obscuring her and gave me a thumb's up with a big smile. "That's my baby," the patient said. "And we're expecting a little one." I replied, "May you enjoy much renewed health—and much freedom," I added. He laughed, and thanked me. I ended with, "And may all that's loving bless you both very much." Correcting myself, I said, "I mean *the three of you.*" "Ah, that's right," he said, laughing.

That patient triggered my own theology: to be free of any religion or ideology that imposes, not empowers. That separates human beings into "natural" and "unnatural." Superior and inferior. Saved and unsaved. Good *versus* evil To be free to transcend divisive dehumanizing stereotypes and embrace one's humanness and rights and that of others may be seen as another form of religion. But there is no need to fit it into a religious classification. One can call it by its real name: "I'm free." Like "Methodism" or "Catholicism," one could call it "Freedomism" or "Freedomist." Or, simply "I'm free." It was enough to make my day—and apparently the patient's and his "baby's" day.

Another patient who made my day is a 91-year-old Pentecostal black woman who found her freedom in Jesus. As soon as I entered her room and identified myself as hospital chaplain, she said, "Oh, pray for me," and began to cry. "You're not doing well?," I asked. "No. Pray for me," she replied. I put my hand on hers, and as soon as I began to pray, she joined in and began to pray loudly in another language, calling forth the spiritual power of her heritage and faith. An ancestral language of clarity and connectedness, I thought. And then her words, "Jesus! Jesus! Jesus! I love you so. Hallelujah! Hallelujah! Hallelujah!," she repeated. I then joined in with, "You heard her, Jesus. She loves you very much." The patient continued to call forth his name again and again in exaltation, and also repeated her evidently empowering chant in what seemed to be her native tongue. At the end of the visit, I said, "I hope you will be feeling better." She replied, "Thank you. Thank you so much for coming."

My presence and response seemed to help this woman call forth, from deep within herself, a cathartic and renewing affirmation of her faith, in the face of her illness and apparent need for human contact. The outpouring of her voice in prayer overflowed, leading me to feel a vicarious reverence for that which affirmed and strengthened her. I did not understand certain of her ancestral words, but their tone of empowerment was clear.

The third patient who made my day is a 64-year-old white woman in an intensive care unit. Her religion was listed as "No Affiliation," which was incorrect. When I asked, she identified herself as a "Christian." Shortly into our conversation, she hesitated, then started to ask me, "What is your religion?" and caught herself and said, "Maybe I'm not allowed to ask that." "You can ask me anything," I replied. "I'm Unitarian and United Methodist, and actually non-sectarian." Then I said, "I encourage you to ask any question of me or of any other staff person here." Upon learning something of who I am, the patient shared more of herself and her family and her independent faith.

The personal mystique of a medical doctor's authority and seeming "aboveness" can create a reverence that may prevent a patient from asking questions important to her or his health, the answers to which often dispel unnecessary anxiety and help facilitate comfort and healing. Questions that a doctor or nurse needs to take the time to encourage and answer, rather than allow any pressure to see a maximum number of patients dictate his or her response. *Making a patient's day depends on giving the patient the time of day.*

Asking questions of any authority is a human right. Answering them is a human responsibility. Questions turn a hierarchical relationship into a more equalitarian relationship. Questions are about rights, equality, and the way democracy works.

While my aim is to make the patient's day as a hospital chaplain, often patients make my day-- with their individuality and insight and humanness and faith.

42. Pastoral Care by Ear and Sight

The 64-year-old black female Baptist patient was put on comfort measures, and her family requested a chaplain. Covering for the chaplains on the other campus, I met her two sons, Charles and John, in the Waiting Room. Unable to hold back his tears, Charles apologized, saying, "I'm the oldest; I should be strong." Tears are not a sign of weakness but of love—growing more endearing with age, ageless not aging. Putting my hand on his shoulder, I replied, "Your tears come from the strength of your love for your mother not from weakness." Charles nodded positively. He then said that the whole family, including an aunt and her son from Arkansas, would be arriving around 4 pm, and asked me to come back then. I was about to begin another pastoral care interaction by ear and eye, this time for 3 ½ hours, with many family members and friends deeply grieving and devotedly supporting their dying loved one.

Much of pastoral care is unscripted. It is about ear and eye. Spontaneous responses to what is heard and seen. Becoming comfortable with silence, seen as natural not awkward. Feeling one does not have to fill it in with talk. Or perform a self-expected conventional ministerial role. Secure around strong emotional expressions of loss, understood as human not as inappropriate or profane. Un-pressured by a fear of not saying the right words. Or of saying the wrong thing. Learning where one is coming from so that one may better know where other people are at. At ease with oneself, and therefore attuned to others.

The family began to gather in the Waiting Room. I made it a point to stand in line and join in as each greeted those arriving. The patient's daughter, Millie, and her teenage son, who has a local music program on an educational television station. The patient's sister, Dorothy and her teenage son from Arkansas. A longtime woman family friend and her daughter. A hospital worker and another woman who also were close family friends. And sons John and Charles, and the latter's wife and her sister.

111

We waited for a long period of time while the nurse attended to the patient. I was able to experience, and when appropriate participate in, the interaction of family members and friends.

The beloved patient's dying led to a family reunion in the Waiting Room, with sharing and reminiscing accompanied by laughter and sighs. Such as the slower driving pace in Arkansas, humorously described by the patient's sister who moved there from Boston several years ago. The inexpensive restaurants there. Which younger son, John, with his love of eating, enjoyed while visiting his Aunt Dorothy. One restaurant after another, non-stop. Patting his stomach, which evoked laughter. The lauding of the patient's expert cooking—for anyone who came to her home. And after a silence, the patient's daughter, Millie, said to me, "How long have you been a chaplain here?" "I'm into my 18th year," I answered. "You must find your work very difficult," she said. I responded, "I have the privilege of meeting different people, like you folks. But at times, yes, I find it sad." She nodded.

As time continued to pass, John, the younger son, asked me, "How long do you stay with a family in this kind of situation?" "As long as the family wants me to," I replied. "We want you to stay," he said, with others echoing his words. "I'm happy to stay," I responded.

The nurse entered the Waiting Room and invited the family to the patient's room. In the room, I observed a family photograph of the patient and her now deceased husband, and in that same photograph, below their photos, the pictures of their two sons and daughter, with stars framing the pictures of the three. I commented on the loving parental affirmation of the three symbolized by the stars.

We gathered around the patient's beside, holding hands as I offered a prayer-- for the patient who, like her creative and renewing god, has passed life on to her children and their children, and who is now surrounded by their abiding love and that of her god.

Her life supports removed, the family and friends drew closer as life slowly ebbed from the patient. The oldest son, Charles, stood over her on one side, wiping her face gently with a tissue, kissing her repeatedly on the cheek, wiping tears from his eyes, and saying, "I love you so much, mother. You're the best mother in the world. I'm going to miss you so." Tearful daughter, Millie, sat on the other side, rubbing her mother's arm, at times laying her head on her mother's bosom and professing her undying love. And younger son, John, looking at the patient, said, "You and I are a lot alike, Mama: we both kid around. Daddy is up there waiting for you, and is wondering why it's taking you so long. I love you, Mama. I love you, Mama." Tears filled his eyes. And other family members and their close friends hugging each other and crying as their loved one died. Sadness also welling up within me.

Like so many other grieving families and friends, this patient and her loved ones reveal that *life is about passing it on.* And pastoral care is about honoring and enabling the passage. It is about staying and being present to the end.

43. "I told God I needed a real flesh and blood angel"

The "very anxious" 63-year-old Latino Catholic female patient was about to undergo the risky coiling of three aneurysms in her brain, but the priest on call was unavailable due to a change in the scheduled surgery. "I will be right over," I told her doctor, who asked if I could come immediately.

I went to the patient's bedside in the Radiology Department, introduced myself, and took her hand; *and she wouldn't let go.* I explained why the priest was unavailable. It seemed to her that no one was available—except an older Spanish-speaking male friend with a cane and a smile, who was sitting beside her.

The patient's daughter in the South was not available. She could not bear to see the sight of her mother connected to machines or hooked up to wires, so she did not come. They talked by telephone. The patient said to her, "How would you feel if I died and you weren't here?" "God would probably send me to hell," her daughter replied, she said. But her nine-year-old granddaughter told her over the telephone, "I'm praying for you, grandma."

Nor were any of the patient's five sisters available, except by telephone. "I'm all alone, and I'm afraid," she said, still firmly holding my hand.

The patient continued, "Why me?" She told her priest, who gave her the Anointing of the Sick the day before, "I'm angry at God." She said that her priest told her, "God can take it. He will understand and forgive you."

Her fear of dying and going to hell herself seemed to lead her to say, "I cared for a dear friend for years, up until he died of cancer. I hope God takes that into account," she added with tears in her eyes, still holding my hand ever so tightly. "That's very loving of you to care for someone like that," I responded, and added, "You are very loving yourself, and very precious to God." The patient seemed to be laboring under a theology of rewards and punishment, heaven and hell—a Pavlovian-like theologically-conditioned response, transmitted by parents, priests and pastors alike to exercise control over people.

The prayer I offered affirmed her god's love for her, gave thanks for her doctors' and nurses' commitment to her well-being, and for her loved ones as well, including the older dear, Spanish-speaking man with the cane sitting at her side. But she was not through with me yet.

After giving her medication in preparation for the aneurysm coiling, the nurse asked her to take the pill she was to have brought with her. "It must be in my bag," she said, and reached for a bag filled with personal items, still holding my right hand with her left hand. All the while holding my hand tight, she engaged in an awkward one-handed search for her bottle of pills. "I got up at 4:30 this morning and had so much to do getting ready to come here," she said, "and I thought I packed everything. But I'm really not together." *Continuing to hold my hand*, she went through a second and then a third bag. Finally she let go of my hand, and used both hands to look for the pills in her pocketbook, and found the bottle.

Upon leaving, I said, "I will come back and see you afterward." She pleaded, "Will you come back? Even if I die, please come." "I'll come back," I said.

I came back, and the patient was very much alive and grateful. And her older Spanish-speaking friend with the cane and the smile was seated in a chair on the other side of her bed. She was sitting on her bed, holding photo x-rays of the aneurysms before and after the coiling. "See, Rev. Alfredo," this is before and this is after it was done." The x-rays showed the large aneurysms before the coiling and three shrunken images of them after. Still looking at the x-rays, the patient said, "Seeing you yesterday meant so much to me. When they were doing it," she continued, "I kept picturing the Chinese doctor's smile and your face. When I woke up, I told them I wanted to see my doctor and Rev. Alfredo." She then looked at my ID badge and said, "I keep calling you Rev. Alfredo. But God understands who I mean." I nodded and smiled.

When I told the patient that I would inform the Catholic chaplain of her presence upon his arrival in the afternoon of the next day, she professed an ecumenical spirit. "I'm not just for one religion," she said. God is one. I go to different churches."

I visited the patient the next day before her noon discharge. Her older male Spanish-speaking friend with the cane and a smile was again sitting by her bedside, and waved a warm hello. The patient began, "You know, Rev. *Alberts* [italics added], I told God I needed a real flesh and blood angel, and he sent me you." I returned her appreciation with a smile, and expressed gratitude for her successful procedure.

I had another mission on this last visit: to understand more about, and possibly affirm, her relationship with her daughter. Recalling the patient's earlier conversation, I said, "Your daughter may feel guilty in saying God would probably send her to hell if you died and she was not here." The patient seemed to understand my concern, saying, "I told her that I wasn't judging her, that I love her unconditionally. While she didn't come, she did send me a robe and slippers for the hospital."

My bringing up the patient's daughter, led her to talk about her own past. Her parents physically abused her when growing up. And her husband used a telephone call to tell her he was leaving and divorcing her for another woman, which left her with two young children to raise on her own. Later she arrived in Boston from the Southwest, by herself and "very anxious." She knew what it was like to have no one available, to be alone, and in need of a "real flesh and blood angel." One is still beside her: an older Spanish-speaking man with a cane and a warm smile. Each time I offered a prayer for her, she asked me to offer a prayer for him too, which I did.

The patient's "Why me?" anger at her god may be seen as a projection of her anger at her abusive father and mother and her husband who were not "available." It was about her not letting go of the hand of a "real flesh and blood angel" who was *available*. "Even if I die, please come back."

Pastoral care is about real "flesh and blood angels" visiting real *flesh and blood* patients.

44. "For the Longest Time"

About to begin my hospital work-day, I was paged and asked to perform the wedding of a 28-year-old white Catholic Hispanic woman patient who was dying of liver failure, and who would be discharged in the afternoon. Because time was short, and I was available, Sister Maryanne Ruzzo, Catholic Chaplain on the patient's campus, asked me to officiate. "I always do a pre-marital conference, Maryanne," I said. "But I modify it to accommodate a given situation."

"That's fine," Maryanne replied. "The groom is in her room. I'll introduce you to them. They are very committed to each other."

The patient-bride, Marie and her 32 year-old Hispanic husband-to be, Carlos have been together for almost three years, and have a 2-year-old son, Carlos, Jr. Marie stopped doing drugs eight years ago, but their terminal effect was revealed in her subdued facial expression and tone of voice. She did not have long to live.

"Why do you want to marry Carlos?" I asked Marie. "Because I love him," she said. Carlos, why do you want to marry Marie?" I continued. "Because I love her," he answered. Some of the most meaningful words are those that directly say, "I love you." Sister Maryanne had already perceived in her relationship with them their strong commitment to each other.

The small chapel on the Menino Pavilion soon filled with nurses and doctors and various other staff who had treated Marie, and others who got word of the wedding. The chapel was buzzing with their excitement in anticipation of this rare, impromptu, wedding event. One staff person bought a beautiful bouquet of purple and white roses for the altar, against which leaned a small smooth wooden crucifix. Another nurse lined up a photographer to take pictures. Other staff bought a big wedding cake for the reception, which was also held in the chapel.

Carlos was wearing a pull-over shirt with a big picture of Roberto Clemente on the front—the great Pittsburgh Pirates National League baseball player who was the first Latin American player elected to the baseball Hall of Fame, and a tremendous humanitarian who died in a December 1972 plane crash while delivering emergency supplies to earthquake victims in Nicaragua.

Marie was wearing a gray top, and a prayer blanket, from Sister Maryanne, covered her legs. And a veil, brought to the hospital for the occasion by a nurse's daughter, crowned the preciousness of her being a bride. She entered the chapel, seated in a wheelchair and was guided toward the front, with Carlos walking beside her. As they processed down the aisle, a nurse, sitting at a piano, played "Here comes the bride." And everyone immediately stood and clapped!

When Marie and Carlos reached the front of the chapel, they, and all of us, were in for a meaningful surprise. Earlier, Sister Maryanne just happened to "find" the Boston University Medical School Choir on the seventh floor singing to patients. The Choir heard of the wedding, and offered to sing an opening song, a piece by Billy Joel. The Choir captured a deep meaning of Marie and Carlos's wedding in singing "For the Longest Time".

Inspired by the Boston University Medical School Choir's singing of Billy Joel's song, I began the wedding ceremony with, "We are gathered here to witness and celebrate the marriage of Marie and Carlos 'for the longest time'."

It was a unique and inspiring wedding in various ways. I turned to the groom and said, "Carlos, do you take Marie to be your wife, to commit yourself to her, 'for the longest time?'" I forgot that Carlos spoke little English. But a bilingual person, picking up on the brief silence, began interpreting my words for Carlos, who then said, "I do."

"Marie, do you take Carlos to be your husband, and commit yourself to him 'for the longest time?,'" I asked. Marie needed no help, answering, "I do." And the same assistance was offered Carlos in the exchanging of their rings.

Next came a Scripture reading by Sister Maryanne, a passage from I Corinthians 13 in the New Testament that also emphasized enduring love:

"If I speak in the tongue of mortals and of angels, but have not love I am a noisy gong or a clanging cymbal. Love is patient; love is kind; Love is not envious or boastful or arrogant or rude. It does not insist on its own way; it is not irritable or resentful; it does not rejoice in wrong-doing, but rejoices in the truth. It bears all things, believes all things, hopes all things, endures all things. Love never ends."

Then came the climatic pronouncement of wife and husband. I

asked Carlos and Marie to join hands, and I put my hand over their hands and declared, "With the authority invested in me by the Commonwealth of Massachusetts, and especially by the authority of your love for each other, I pronounce you husband and wife together 'for the longest time'." When Marie and Carlos then kissed, everyone in the chapel enthusiastically clapped with much delight.

Sister Maryanne ended the wedding ceremony by putting her hands on Marie and Carlos's heads, and singing a Biblical blessing in a melodic voice: "May the Lord bless and keep you, and let God's grace shine upon you. May God show love so kindly and give you peace and strength. Amen." All of us then gathered around Marie and Carlos, congratulating them and wishing them much happiness-- aware of Marie's impending death. She died two days later.

A wedding cake, and laughter, and energy, and love and tears. A celebration of life and love. It is not about how short a time Marie and Carlos would be together but about how long. Life is about love that lasts "for the longest time." Health care is about protecting and nourishing life "for the longest time." Pastoral care is about affirming and enabling the fulfillment of every patient's life "for the longest time."

45. "No Preference"

He was a husky 48-year-old black patient, who had his gall bladder removed, and whose religion was listed "VERIFIED NO AFFILIATION" -- a classification I usually check as it may not be accurate. "Hi, Mr. Jackson. I'm Rev. Alberts, Hospital Chaplain, making my rounds on the floor. Your religion is listed as 'No Affiliation.' Is that correct?" "I told them [Admitting Department] 'no preference'," he replied. I was to discover an unusual theological meaning of "no preference".

"What does 'no preference' mean to you?" I asked. The patient explained: "I was in the Marines for five years. And, regarding religion, written on my dog tags were the words, 'no preference'. If I were killed, I didn't care which chaplain stood over me. I figured that all of them represented the same god, since there's just one god."

He went from theological clarity to psychological awareness. "Other Marines would see 'no preference' written on my dog tags and think, 'Oh, oh. He's against religion. He doesn't believe in God.' That's not true. If they had inquired, like you just did, they would have found out what 'no preference' really means. I believe there's one god that people call by different names."

The patient also verbalized political understanding. "You know, I was in the Marines. There is always one war or another, you know, supposedly to help everyone. You go fight for someone else's benefit." He knew. In America's white-controlled society, the only place many people of color can 'Be all you can be' is in the Army—sadly with the current recession a rich boon for poor black—and white—recruits. With the armaments and reconstruction and energy industries—and power-seeking, fear-mongering politicians-- the benefactors of perpetual war.

The patient continued to demonstrate theological insight. "My grandmother is 94 years old and quite ill," he said. "I cannot ask God to keep her alive. If He did that for me, that would make me godly. And people might begin praying to me and not to Him. And that would be foolishness."

While stressing 'no preference', the patient stated that he was a Christian, and responded positively when I asked if he would like me to offer a prayer. I began, "God of love," then forgot the patient's name, and stopped, and began searching for it on my patient list. Finally, I said to him, "I forgot your name, and am trying to find it on my patient list. Ah, there it is: Robert Jackson." He waited. I began again: "God of love. You know each of our names, and want us to know and remember each other's name. We thank you for loving all of us equally instead of having a preference. And I thank you for Robert Jackson..."

46. "Here comes the bill collector"

"Here comes the bill collector," the 79-year-old white patient, sitting in a chair near his wife, jokingly said as I entered his intensive care unit room. "I am the bill collector," I replied, smiling, and added, ""Well, that's partly true. My name is Bill. I'm Bill Alberts, hospital chaplain, making my rounds on the floor." We were about to make each other's day.

I explained, "I'm just checking to verify that you are not affiliated with a religion. "That's right," he said. He then made a statement that went to the heart of religion for me. "I think all people should believe as they choose. But I don't think one group's religion is right and another's is wrong. People should not try to impose their beliefs on others. That is part of the problem with the world today."

"What else is the problem of the world?" I asked.

"Politicians! I hate politicians," he said. "Most are just interested in getting power, and then lining their pockets with money from special interests groups, rather than representing the people. In time, even the good ones compromise their ethics."

His comments resonated with me. But as the hospital chaplain, I usually kept such opinions to myself.

"You have a tough job," he said. "It has its moments," I responded, "but people like you make it very interesting." "You probably like visiting people like me who are not affiliated with a religion." "I do," I said, smiling.

He was enjoying the visit too, as was his wife. "You look really great," he said. "Do you always have to dress up like that?" (I was wearing a light tan sport coat and dark brown slacks, with matching tie and shirt.) "It goes with the job," I answered. "You look spiffy," he said. I gave credit to my wife and daughters for selecting my shirts and ties, and added, with another smile, "I'm left-handed. So I'm kind of awkward at that kind of thing." The patient's wife then made an astute observation: "You'd look the same whether you were dressed up or not." "Probably so," I said.

An apparent role of the patient's wife was to keep him honest. At one point, he said that he himself was a relatively agreeable person. "Except on occasion," his wife said with a smile. "Except when I don't agree with her," he replied, returning the smile. Then he seemed to want to impress his wife: "Let's see. We've been married fifty, ah, fifty, ah," he hesitated, then said, "fifty-six years," looking at her. "Fifty-five years," she said.

Semi-retired, the patient is in the "seafood business, worldwide." "You've heard of scallops," he said. "I love scallops," I responded. "Too bad I did not know that before I came here," he said. "The next time you can pay the bill in scallops, "I jokingly said. "I'll do that," he answered laughing.

Before leaving, I expressed appreciation for the patient's statement that all people have a right to believe as they chose, and should respect each other's religious beliefs. I then shook his hand. He said, "Thank you. You made my day." I replied, "You made my day, too."

It is revealing how *democratic* certain non-religious professing patients appear to be.

47. "Would you bless this crucifix for me?"

She was a 79-year-old black Catholic patient, whose heart arrested and who was just admitted to the Emergency Room. The mother of a hospital staff person who taught me computer skills early on and who also resolved a dispute that enabled another employee to become more effective in her work. A concerned nurse, whom I've known for years, alerted me to the presence of the gravely ill patient, and to her family in the waiting room. I followed the progress of the patient from the Emergency Room to the Intensive Care Unit, providing welcomed pastoral care for her family and for her, and informing the two Catholic chaplains of the patient's presence and her relationship to the long-time staff person. The patient and family were appreciative of the Catholic chaplains' visits and prayers, and one of them anointed her. It was her request of me that came as a complete surprise.

Her critical condition having improved, she was sitting on a chair in the Intensive Care Unit. When I entered and we exchanged greetings, she pulled open a drawer in the stand facing her, took out a small, old wooden crucifix and asked, "Would you bless this crucifix for me?" I thought I heard her unexpected request correctly, but still asked to be sure: "What did you say?" "Would you bless this for me?"

Pastoral care boundaries help to guide my work. Inter-faith collegiality involves us chaplains recognizing and affirming and facilitating each other's care of patients and their families—with the wishes of patients and their families paramount. Thus, I said to the Catholic patient, "Mrs. Martin, do you know that I am a minister and not a priest?" "I know that," she replied. I then said, "I'd be happy to bless your crucifix."

I took the worn wooden crucifix from her, held it up in my hand, and began, "God of love, as you bless this crucifix, you also bless Mrs. Martin with your love." I continued: "We thank you for this crucifix, as it reminds us of Jesus, who reminds us of your love for every one of us. We thank you for all of the reminders of your love. And as you bless this crucifix, we thank you for all that blesses and nourishes and renews Mrs. Martin. We also thank you for all that blesses her family as well. Amen"

After the blessing, Mrs. Martin said, "My daughter got this crucifix for me in Mexico. Twenty years ago," she lovingly added. A reminder of a daughter's love. A reminder of divine love.

That same day, while visiting another patient in the Intensive Care Unit, a nurse came to me and said, "When you are through, you are wanted in Mrs. Martin's room." When I entered, two of her daughters were there, and one of them said, "My mother wants you to bless this Rosary." It gave me the opportunity to call forth a blessing I had omitted with the crucifix: "God of love, as you bless this Rosary, we also give you thanks for the blessing of love that Mrs. Martin and her daughters and sons have for each other."

48. Go Down Kicking

Frank McGuire was a 51-year-old white United Methodist minister dying of pancreatic cancer, who wanted to share a message with people, but was too weak to put his thoughts on paper. So I volunteered to write down what he wanted to say. We did not meet in the hospital, but in his home in Virginia where I drove to see him. The year was 1991. A social worker as well as a minister, Frank and I were longtime close friends. We did street work together night after night during the summer of 1968, when thousands of so-called "hippies" flocked to the Boston Common. Having grown up in a tough neighborhood in St. Louis, Frank was most effective in diffusing tension, breaking up fights, and stabilizing violence-prone situations. And now he wanted to share with people the biggest fight of his life.

Frank had great difficulty communicating to me what he wanted to tell people. He had been tall and stocky, but was now extremely thin and weak and his hair prematurely white. At times, during our conversation, his voice would grow faint and fade and his eyes would close.

"One of the things I always feared was cancer," Frank began. "When the doctor told me that a CAT scan revealed I had pancreatic cancer in a very advanced stage and only had six months, plus or minus, to live, I was naturally scared. But there wasn't anything I could do about it except determine my attitude."

Frank's attitude was one of the messages he wanted to share with people. "I could either roll over and die, and some people literally do that. Or I could acquiesce, go along with it, not do much of anything, give in. Or I could fight it, *go down kicking*. I was determined I wasn't going to die just by giving up. No matter what the quality of life was toward the end," he continued, "it was still more important than not having any life. The more you give in the less quality you have."

When I asked what he meant by quality of life, Frank responded, "Enjoyability. Just having more fun in any way you can. Whether it be a day trip, watching a movie, listening to a piece of music, learning new things." He even "tried to learn how to operate a Macintosh Computer." His point: "If you are obsessed with what you are not able to do, you will be blind to the new opportunities."

Throughout my visit, Frank struggled against the adverse effects of the medicine he took to ease his pain. "There are days when it's rough," he said. "Two days ago I woke up and felt like I didn't have any coping mechanisms whatsoever. There are certain unknowns." Frank hesitated, groping for words. He welled up. "You don't have much strength. You're weaker. And you worry." He stopped and broke down. I did not know what to say to comfort him. Trying to push aside my own uneasiness and hesitation, I reached out and held his hand. After a moment, he continued through sobs, "You worry about how much time you have left. And yet the one thing I try to balance that off with is that there's no sense of worrying how much time you don't have left. It's more important," he said, "to deal with what you do have left. You could become awfully morose and despairing."

Frank regained his composure. "No matter how bad things work, there are still things that are good. And to not get stuck worrying that you may be at the end of your life. That you know is close. Probably not as close as you are feeling. It's close." He then said, "Do the best you can and the most that you can, because there will come a time when you won't be able to do that."

Frank wanted to tell people that the most important possession they have is life itself. "So often I hear a person say, 'Life isn't worth a damn.' I would ask him what he would do if he went to a doctor this afternoon and was told, 'Mr. Jones, you have two months to live. How would you live it?' I would tell him to think about everything he would like to do, and do as many of them within the possibilities of time and finances. I would tell him to keep living." I responded, "That's what you have been doing, Frank."

Frank also wanted to share with people his understanding of faith. "My life takes its course from an understanding of God as Creator," he said. "God does not cause cancer. Having cancer does not mean unfaithfulness. God," he continued, "wants us to live, not die. I think God wants us to reach our potential no matter what the circumstances are." He then said, "I believe that God wants people to be able to forgive themselves for what they may feel guilty about rather than continue punishing themselves. I also think God would want people to walk humbly, love their neighbor, do justice."

Frank himself gave flesh and blood meaning to the prophetic

message of "preaching good news to the poor." As Chairperson of Social Work for Area 2 of Fairfax County (Virginia) Public Schools, he helped to established a breakfast program for poor immigrant children in one school, which led other schools in the Area to adopt the program. Frank said, "A kid who comes to school with an empty stomach is not apt to pay attention and learn as well." Frank was making an important point: *a full stomach feeds a hungry mind.*

Frank saw my writing down what he wanted to tell people as "one of the last ministries I could do. I would like to give people a message of hope," he explained. "Don't despair when you are confronted with a debilitating or life-threatening disease. You can go on. The sun comes up each day whether you can see it or not. We can be part of that sunrise. It gives us another opportunity to deal with obstacles." He concluded, "Not all has ended. I hope that people will be able to find within themselves the ability to see there is a glowing light to tap into that could help them."

A few weeks later when I called Frank to discuss the first draft of what I had written, his wife, Judy, answered the telephone with sad news. "Frank died this morning," she said. During a subsequent telephone conversation, Judy talked about a trip Frank and she took three months earlier to the Red Woods in California and Crater Lake in Oregon. She stated, "Frank always wanted to go to Crater Lake, as it is one of the most impressive sights you would want to see. TWA was offering $99 tickets to San Francisco and Los Angeles, so we went." She then said, "We drove for eight days in California and Oregon. No matter how sick Frank was, he wound himself up to do that. They said he would be dead in six months," she went on, "but he was traveling in California and sending post cards back home to people. He got a kick out of that."

Rev. Franklin W. McGuire, MSW, is his real name.

49. It Is About Kindness

As I entered the eight floor hospital unit, a 59-year-old black Catholic patient was sitting just outside her room, crying. She looked at me from a distance, and, in her desperation, repeated what she asked everyone she could lay her eyes on: "Would you walk me down the hall?" I told her that I could not do that, then went to her and said that she should request that of her nurse. Evidently assuming that I was a chaplain, she said that she would like to receive communion. I told her that I would share her request with any Eucharistic Minister I might see. "And I hope you will be feeling better," I said. "Thank you," she said.

When I returned to the unit's center after visiting another patient, I observed a black staff person in her fifties stopping and talking with the patient who was crying. I was struck by her kindness toward the patient. "Look here, girl," she said in a sisterly way, "I want you to stop crying. I'm going to come back, and comb your hair. Okay? I'll check what is down the hall, and come back, and we can talk. No more gray eyes. Bright eyes and a smile," she added, with a smile of her own, seeking to bolster the patient's spirit. "Alright," the patient said appreciatively, and stopped crying.

Shortly, a longtime, caring, white, Catholic Eucharistic Minister, who had been a nurse all her adult life, entered the unit. I told her that the patient was upset, and had requested communion. The Eucharistic Minister walked over to the patient, introduced herself, and asked, "Would you like to receive communion?" "Yes," the patient replied. The Eucharistic Minister said, "I hope you will be feeling better," and served her communion.

No sooner had the patient received communion, than the black staff woman returned from down the hall, with breakfast on a plate for the patient. The staff person then proceeded to bend over and cut the patient's food for her. From spiritual food for the soul to physical food for the body—both of which evidently warmed the patient's heart.

The staff person's kindness led me to introduce myself to her later, and say, "I really appreciate what you are doing for that patient." "Well, thank you! Thank you!" she replied, with a big smile "Anytime!"

Palestinian-American poet Naomi Shihab Nye had people like this vulnerable patient—and her caregivers, and all of us—in mind in her poem on "Kindness":

> Before you know what kindness really is
> You must lose things,
> feel the future dissolve in a moment
> like salt in a weakened broth.
> What you held in your hand,
> what you counted and carefully saved,
> all this must go so you know
> how desolate the landscape can be
> between the regions of kindness.
> How you ride and ride
> thinking the bus will never stop,
> the passengers eating maize and chicken
> will stare out the window forever.
>
> Before you learn the tender gravity of kindness,
> you must travel where the Indian in a white poncho
> lies dead by the side of the road.
> You must see how this could be you,
> how he too was someone
> who journeyed through the night with plans
> and the simple breath that kept him alive.
>
> Before you know kindness as the deepest thing inside,
> you must know sorrow as the other deepest thing.
> You must wake up with sorrow.
> You must speak to it till your voice
> catches the thread of all sorrows
> and you see the size of the cloth.
>
> Then it is only kindness that makes sense anymore,
> only kindness that ties your shoes
> and sends you out into the day to mail letters and
> purchase bread,
> only kindness that raises its head
> from the crowd of the world to say

it is I you have been looking for,
and then goes with you every where
like a shadow or a friend.
I was privileged to observe these acts of kindness by a staff person and a Eucharistic Minister. Kindness that may go unnoticed but may be seen anywhere "anytime." Pastoral care is about embodying and facilitating and revering kindness.

50. "I'll take what you've got"

What I assumed would be a routine visit, asking a 64-year-old black patient if she were affiliated with a religion, turned out to be the highlight of my day—and possibly of her day.

"I'm Rev. Alberts, hospital chaplain, making my rounds," I began, "and your religion is listed as 'Unknown.'" The patient, surrounded by her daughter and her sister and her 52-year-old Hispanic roommate (whom, coincidentally, she has known for years), said that she no longer attends her church. Nor do her daughter and her sister attend the church anymore. The patient, however, welcomed me into her room with, "But we'll take what you got!" which led her daughter and her sister and her roommate to burst out laughing. "Better yet," I replied with a smile, "I'll take what you've got!" They responded with more laughter, which increased in delight when I added, "You're where it's at." With my response still drawing chuckles, the patient said, "Well come on in and sit down with us then!" pointing to an empty chair in front of her bed. I sat down, and the four of them began to tell me where they were "at."

First the patient's roommate-friend. I was pleasantly surprised to learn that she and the patient have been longtime friends. When I noted that she was listed Catholic, she said where she and her god were "at." "God's everywhere," she said, adding, "and for all of us."

The patient's daughter began to explain where she and her mother and her aunt were "at." "The devil has interrupted our church, and that's why we don't go anymore," she said. Seeking to understand what she was driving at, I asked, "How has the devil interrupted your church?" The daughter responded, "Well, there is worldliness and godliness; and when you go to church you expect godliness and not worldliness. But you go to church and it's the same worldliness there as outside."

I continued to pursue what the daughter was getting at: "Could you give me an example of what you mean by 'worldliness'?" The daughter struggled briefly for the words, and then began to get into a

132

sensitive subject: "Well, ah, you don't expect the pastor to be fooling around. Ah, it's infidelity. He's sleeping with other women. And that's not right." The patient's sister added, "And the pastor's son is the organist, and he's fooling around with little boys"—rolling her eyes to tell me what she meant.

The daughter said, "Church is in your heart," placing her hand over her heart. "You don't have to go to a building." I readily affirmed her words, that belief is a matter of the heart. The daughter echoed the feelings of her mother, who still sees herself as a Christian.

The patient and her daughter and sister and friend responded positively to my offer of prayer. I prayed to a god who, as the patient's roommate and friend said, "is everywhere" and "for all of us," to a god whose altar, as the daughter said, is the human heart, and to a god who loves everyone, and to whom we give thanks for all that affirms and renews the patient and her roommate.

After the prayer, the patient's daughter said, "Oh, could you say another prayer, for my sister?" "Sure," I said. "What would you like me to pray about her?" "She's very confused right now." "About what?" I asked. "Just about everything," she replied. "She's having a hard time. Pray that she gets understanding." I prayed for her sister, using her own words, and then gave thanks for the concern and love of this daughter for her sister. When I finished, they all clapped, which greatly surprised me.

Pastoral care is not about where the hospital chaplain's "at" and what he or she's "got" to bestow, but about where patients and their loved ones are "at" and what they've "got" to share.

51. Homeless But Not Loveless

It was Christmas Eve. I was the hospital chaplain on call, and the page came at 10:15 pm: the intensive care unit secretary said, "The patient is dying; she is going to be taken off the ventilator, and they want a prayer."

The medically paralyzed patient, Millie, was a homeless white woman in her forties. Those who "want a prayer" were her bearded boyfriend, Kenneth, also homeless, and her older sister and brother-in-law. Kenneth and Millie met at a homeless shelter nine months ago.

Kenneth was standing on one side of the bed holding Millie's hand, and her sister was seated on the other side, rubbing her arm, with her husband seated next to her, and I was standing near him. I had offered the prayer they had requested.

The removal of the ventilator tube led Kenneth and Millie's sister and brother-in-law to intensify their loving support. Homeless himself for four years, Kenneth drew closer and stroked Millie's brow; and her sister repeatedly whispered into her ear: "I'm here, Millie. I'm here. I love you, Millie. I love you," At this point the husband began to rub his wife's shoulder, and she turned and kissed his hand. Love flowed from one through the other to the other.

When it passed midnight, Millie's sister suggested that we find a Christmas service on television. I located one, with a church choir singing, "O holy night." We were deeply involved in a holy night of love.

After considerable time passed, I went over and stood beside Kenneth and asked if he would like to sit in my chair. "No. I'm okay," he said. "I'm used to it. In the last few years I watched my mother and brother and uncle and aunt die." Then he thought about what he had just said, and reflected, "Well, you don't get used to it." His watery eyes told the same story.

The older sister then lovingly affirmed Kenneth. She expressed great appreciation for his relationship with Millie: "My sister has had little happiness in her life. I'm so thankful that she and Kenneth found each other. These last nine months have been her happiest, for which I am so grateful." She then held Kenneth's face in her hands, and he responded by putting his hands to her face in a moving expression of gratitude and love. I commented that her words were a beautiful testimony to Kenneth's relationship with Millie.

A few moments after Millie died, her mother called from Florida. The older daughter said, "She just passed away, mother. What? You want me to put my cell phone to her ear? She's gone, mother. Alright, I'll do it." With that, she put the phone next to her dead sister's ear so that her mother could say whatever words of love and regret that might bring her relief and comfort. Evidently the older daughter heard her mother's pain: upon taking the phone from Millie's ear, she immediately said, "Are you alright, mother? Are you alright, mother? We've been here with Millie all of the time, mother. She died peacefully. She knows you love her."

In my more than 17 years as a hospital chaplain, I have been present at many such "holy nights" (and days) of human love expressed by so many culturally and religiously and politically and economically diverse people: "Don't go, Mamma. Don't leave me. I love you, Mamma." "You were always here for me, Dad. I will always love you." "God damn it! I love her so!" So many human expressions. Love's universal grieving after-shocks: anguish and anger, crying and cursing, screaming and shaking, silent and solemn, stroking and hugging and comforting. Human love transcends culture and color, religious belief and political ideology, poverty and wealth, straight and lesbian and gay and bisexual and transgender. People with less love as deeply as people with more. As with birth, death reveals the humanness all of us share, and love is the heart of that humanness. To hear each other's laughter and to see each other's tears is to experience each other's humanness.

Homeless but not loveless.

52. She Made Something Out of Nothing

The 75-year-old, slight, black Methodist woman laid still, in death, on that hospital bed. Looking at her, one might not be aware that such a small body had housed a giant spirit. A spirit filled with courage, power and love, to which her son, Charles, testified, as he sat next to her and I next to him.

"We came from Honduras 30 years ago," he began. "My mother gathered my brother and sister and I together and said, 'We're going to America to find a better life.'" They had nothing. Yet, she made something out of nothing.

As Charles was talking, I looked at his frail, lifeless mother on that hospital bed, and began to sense how great a human being she must have been. When she and her family arrived in America, she did not speak English. Nor did she know the culture. How many lines did she have to wait in? How many times did she have to ask people for directions—and for information? How many jobs did she apply for—and do at one time or another to feed and clothe her family? How often did she feel, or was made to feel, like an outsider? How often must she have turned to her god for comfort and affirmation and strength?

Charles continued, "She worked hard to put food on the table and pay the bills. She was a good mother. She loved us very much. She did not raise thieves or robbers. She took pride in her children and in her home. She took us to church every Sunday. She was a great cook, and welcomed everyone to her table."

Charles then talked about his own struggle to pay the bills. With his mother's help, he attended an auto mechanic school; and has been an auto repair worker for 30 years. Ironically, to save money, instead of driving a car to the auto repair shop, some 30 miles from home, he takes the bus. He rides the bus everywhere, including to the hospital to see his mother. He saves on car insurance and gas and upkeep. He is treading water financially, with much pressure to make ends meet. He has a wife and three children, and is still seeking that better life in America. He is one of millions of invisible, hardworking people for whom life is no "tea party."

After listening to Charles' story and offering a prayer that affirmed his mother's eternal preciousness, I wished him much success in his work, saying, "May you make enough money to pay your bills and some extra as well to give you security." He replied, "Even more important than that is being close to my family." His mother had loved him well.

53. A Christmas Story: "Ah, I can see a little sparkle now"

Christmas was a few days away, and the patient I was about to visit was to put one of its meanings literally in my hand. She is a small, 91-year-old white patient sitting on a chair by her bed, with her daughter in another chair reading a book. "I'm Rev. Alberts, Hospital Chaplain making my rounds," I said with a smile. The patient, not relaxing her stare, ordered, "Sit down and talk to me." Her daughter responded by immediately giving her chair to me, and then sat on the bed. I pulled the chair up closer to the patient as my aim was to possibly establish some closeness with her.

"You're listed as a Christian," I said. "What does that mean?" she demanded. "Whatever it means to you," I replied. "I don't go to church," she said. Her daughter then explained, "Mom was a Catholic, and my dad was an Episcopalian, and my sister and I were raised Episcopalian. So I listed her as Christian." I responded to the patient, "I assume that is what it means to you then." She continued to stare at me.

I moved to the patient's condition: "How are you doing today?" "Not good at all," she replied. "I hate hospitals. I don't want to be in this damn place." I answered, "If you hate hospitals, I can see why you don't want to be here. My father hated doctors. But the hospital is a good place to be when you need the treatment it provides." Her look indicated my common sense was neither informing nor comforting.

The patient's daughter was again very helpful: "Mom has lived alone for 20 years, ever since dad died. And until now, at age 91, she has *never* been in a hospital. Three days ago she fell and broke her hip in three places, and is in a lot of pain. And now she is sitting in a chair, which is remarkable." "I can see why you don't like it here, with your pain and what you're dealing with," I said, and added, "But it's still a good place to help with the healing." She replied, "People